*"I want you to know—not just believe, but **know**, to the core of your spirit where the truth lives—that you are eternal...."*

—from *Past Lives, Future Healing*

Praise for Sylvia Browne

"Psychic, Medium, Clairvoyant, Channel—these are all words to describe Sylvia Browne's unique powers. I've personally witnessed her bring closure to distraught families, help the police close cases, and open people's hearts to help them see the good within themselves."

—Montel Williams

"*The Other Side and Back* is the most grounded and authentic 'entry to the other side' that I have ever read. You know immediately upon reading the first few pages that Sylvia Browne is more than a psychic—she is a master at conveying the truth that exists in the fourth dimension."

—Caroline Myss, Ph.D.,
author of *Anatomy of the Spirit*

SYLVIA BROWNE

WITH
LINDSAY HARRISON

PAST LIVES,
FUTURE
HEALING

A Psychic Reveals the
Secrets of Good Health and
Great Relationships

NEW AMERICAN LIBRARY

NEW AMERICAN LIBRARY
Published by New American Library, a division of
Penguin Putnam Inc., 375 Hudson Street,
New York, New York 10014, U.S.A.
Penguin Books Ltd, 80 Strand,
London WC2R 0RL, England
Penguin Books Australia Ltd, Ringwood,
Victoria, Australia
Penguin Books Canada Ltd, 10 Alcorn Avenue,
Toronto, Ontario, Canada M4V 3B2
Penguin Books (N.Z.) Ltd, 182–190 Wairau Road,
Auckland 10, New Zealand

Penguin Books Ltd, Registered Offices:
Harmondsworth, Middlesex, England

Published by New American Library, a division of Penguin Putnam Inc.
Previously published in a Dutton edition.

First New American Library Printing, June 2002
10 9 8 7 6 5 4 3 2 1

(NAL) REGISTERED TRADEMARK—MARCA REGISTRADA

New American Library Trade Paperback ISBN: 0-451-20597-9

The Library of Congress has catalogued the hardcover edition of this book as
follows:
Browne, Sylvia.
Past lives, future healing : a psychic reveals the secrets of good health and great
relationships / by Sylvia Browne with Lindsay Harrison.
p.   cm.
ISBN 0-525-94606-3 (alk. paper)
1. Reincarnation. 2. Reincarnation therapy. I. Harrison, Lindsay. II. Title.
BL515.B769 2001
133.9'01'35—dc21   2001028720

Set in Perpetua
Designed by Eve L. Kirch
Printed in the United States of America

Dedications

from Sylvia:

To Lindsay Harrison,
who is not only my dearest friend and cowriter
but also my kindred soul.
And to all the loved ones,
here and on The Other Side,
who have believed in me.

from Lindsay:

To *my* kindred soul, Sylvia Browne,
who, by writing her dedication first,
left me with nothing to say but "ditto,"
and the added understatement,
from me and from countless others,
"Thank God for you."

Contents

Introduction

THIS BOOK WILL CLARIFY how every day of the life you're living now is affected, through the power of a force called cell memory, by the lives you've lived before.

In it you'll discover exactly how and why cell memory works.

You'll read story after story after story of my clients' trips back in time to uncover the sources of some of their deepest problems and some of their greatest unexpressed talents and joys.

And through the stories you'll find the key to changing your life dramatically for the better, starting today, by unlocking your own cell memories, embracing the ones that will enrich you, and releasing the ones that have been weighing you down for longer than you might ever have imagined.

These stories were selected from literally thousands of regressions I've done in my twenty-five years of intensive past lives and cell-memory studies. While every story is true and documented, I want to make it very clear that my clients' privacy and anonymity are sacred to me, and not one of their real names has been used in this book.

I also want to add a note to the skeptics and critics who seem so eager to pounce on every book about spirituality, past lives, and those of us who believe so passionately and surely that one of God's promises to each of us at the moment of our creation was, is, and always will be the eternal survival of the soul:

Please, by all means, be skeptical. Be critical. I don't just welcome it, I encourage it, as long as you approach these subjects and those of us who write about them with an open mind, and as long as, in your dismissal, you offer society something equally credible, hopeful, comforting, and reverent to believe instead. By all means, let's sit down at a table, face-to-face, with cameras rolling if you like, and talk. I'll bring my forty-eight years of study, research, readings, past-life regressions, world travel, and comparative religion courses. I'll bring my intensive exploration of twenty-six versions of the Bible as well as the teachings of Buddha and Mohammed, the Koran, the *Egyptian Book of the Dead*, the *Bhagavad Gita*, the works of everyone from Carl Jung to Joseph Campbell to Edgar Cayce to Harold Bloom to Elaine Pagels to Eileen Garrett to the life of Apollonius of Tyana and the philosophies of the Essenes, the Shinto, the Theosophical Society, and the Rosicrucians. And last but certainly not least, I'll bring a genuine interest in your point of view, an honest life devoting the gifts God gave me to His service the best way I know how, and a belief that you might have something of value to teach me. If you'll bring something other than your cynicism, please consider this a standing invitation from me and a meeting I'll look forward to.

In case you're wondering—and you easily could be—where this outburst is coming from, I should tell you that I was recently in the midst of taping an interview for a popular television magazine-format news program when one of the producers happened to mention the two psychiatrists they were including in my segment, who felt that all my work and writing about The Other Side and the spirit world and past lives is actually harmful to society because these are just "feel-good fantasies for the mind to postpone and interfere with the grieving process." I said I was glad they'd invited whoever these two psychiatrists were (I was never told their names) and would enjoy talking to them. Imagine my chagrin when I was told that no, I wouldn't be meeting them, or talking to them. They'd be brought on at the end of the segment—in other words, after I'd finished—to offer their "opposing points of view." I asked the producer to reconsider, to let me at least meet and face my "accusers" to debate their issues and rebut their arguments, but no, that was out of the question. "Not good television," I think was the way he put it. And with that, I thanked them for thinking of me, ended the interview, and walked out.

Because I can't handle criticism? Hardly. After half a century as a very public, outspoken psychic, I doubt if there's criticism I haven't heard or an accusation I haven't run up against. In fact, for reasons I have yet to figure out, it's become very popular in the last year or so for total strangers to walk up to me on the street, or especially in a restaurant when I'm trying to have a quiet dinner, and say, "Wow, I never thought you'd be so beautiful in person. You're so ugly on TV." I have a long list of witnesses who will swear that it makes me laugh every time. But will I insist on a chance to respond to that criticism, instead of giving the last word to some "expert" who's never met me, doesn't know me, and hasn't given me the courtesy of a one-on-one discussion? You bet I will. And if you really want to make any humanitarian's hair stand on end, accuse them of doing something "harmful to society."

No, false hope is harmful to society. What I've offered in my other books, and what I offer in this one, is what I believe with all my heart and soul, to the core of my spirit, to be—literally—the God's honest truth.

There's a quote by Teddy Roosevelt (why am I tempted to add "of all people"?) that I love and keep near me at all times, and I want to share it with you, not just on my behalf but on yours as well, because I believe it's a gorgeous message for all of us to remember and live by:

> *"It is not the critic who counts, not the man who points out how the strong man stumbled or where the doer of good deeds could have done better.*
>
> *The credit belongs to the man who is actually in the arena; whose face is marred by dust and sweat and blood; who strives valiantly; who errs and comes short again and again; who knows the great enthusiasms, the great devotions, and spends himself in a worthy cause; who at the best knows in the end the triumph of high achievement; and who at the worst, if he fails, at least fails while daring greatly, so that his place shall never be with those cold and timid souls who know neither victory nor defeat."*

To my beloved family, friends, ministers, clients, audiences, colleagues, those of the above who are still to come, and to the *open-minded* skeptics everywhere beside whom I stand proudly in that arena, I thank you, I love you, and God bless you.

Sylvia C. Browne

PART ONE

The Mysteries of Cell Memory

PROLOGUE

I<small>T WAS DARK AND COLD</small>, the end of a long day, and I hoped as I left my office that I'd make it home before the approaching storm arrived. I was saying good night to my staff when I noticed that my assistant Michael was on a call that was clearly troubling him. He looked at me, mouthed the name of a client I remembered fondly from a few years back, and pantomimed that she was crying. I stepped back into my office, closed the door, and picked up the phone, barely noticing the low rumble of thunder that shook the window beside me. "Robin, it's Sylvia."

"Oh, Sylvia, thank God I got through to you. You're my last hope. Or should I say *our* last hope. It's about my husband." I could hear the fear in her voice as a disturbing story spilled out of her. It seems that one day four years earlier her husband, Rick, a successful landscape architect, had headed out for a routine trip to the grocery store, returned without groceries a half hour later in an absolute panic, shut himself in their bedroom, and had essentially refused to leave the house ever since. He couldn't explain this sudden, desperate agoraphobia to himself, let alone to her or to the battery of doctors and psychiatrists she'd begged him to see, and after thousands of dollars worth of treatment and medication, he wasn't one bit better. His terror of leaving the house had naturally cost him his clientele and his career; they were on the verge of bankruptcy. As much as she'd loved the man she'd married ten years ago, Robin wasn't sure she could go on living with this frightened recluse she seemed unable to help. "Please, Sylvia," she pleaded through her tears, "I can't take this anymore, and neither can he. In fact, if this goes on much longer, I'm afraid he might try to take his own life. You know I trust you, so just tell me what to do and I'll do it."

"Can you get him to come here?" I asked.

"Forget 'can,' I *will*," she told me. "When?"

"Now. Right away. I'll wait for you."

Three hours later Rick and I were alone in my office while a hard rain fell outside. He was shockingly pale, with the gaunt look of someone whose once-healthy body had taken on more stress than it could handle, and his gray eyes looked haunted by a dark, soul-wrenching fear. Like most clients who genuinely want to be helped, he let me lead him easily into a deep hypnotic trance and take him back to the grocery store trip four years earlier that seemed to have triggered his breakdown. It sounded unremarkable until he frowned slightly and added, "Oh, and there was this little boy in the produce department."

I asked what the little boy was doing.

"He took an apple and started to bite into it. But his father ran over to him yelling, 'Don't eat that without washing it, it might poison you!' "

Poison. A potentially traumatic word. I jotted it on my notepad while calmly asking, "And did that mean something special to you?"

There was a long silence before he realized, "I'd forgotten about this, but yes, it did. I was four years old, and my family was on a vacation in Mexico. There were some kids playing beside the water in a drainage ditch, or sewage ditch or something, and I went over to play with them, but suddenly my dad grabbed me and hollered at the top of his lungs, 'Don't touch that water, it's poison!' I remember it scared me to death at the time."

Poison again. Twice in one lifetime. And a father and young son as well. I didn't have to be psychic, or even all that bright, to link those two events. But a parent's admonition to a four-year-old, no matter how loud and dramatic, doesn't necessarily frighten the child that deeply. So I repeated, "And did *that* mean something special to you? Let yourself go farther back, see if you can step past the veil of this life and tell me what if anything happens." As strongly as I felt that something else was buried in his spirit's memory, I couldn't help him by leading him to it. He had to find it on his own.

"My skin," he finally said.

"What about your skin, Rick?"

"It's brown. Golden brown."

"Are you male, or female?"

"I'm male. Tall. Very muscular. My hair is long and black, and I have large brown eyes."

"Where are you?"

"South America. Near the coast. On a high hilltop. I can see the ocean in the distance from the courtyard of my house where I'm sitting."

"What's the year?"

Without hesitation he answered, "Fourteen hundred eleven."

"Are you alone?"

He shook his head. "My advisers are with me. I'm Aztec. A ruler. Royalty. We're being served a meal. There's tension. A lot of tension. No one's speaking. The only sound is all of us eating. I can hear our metal goblets on the stone table."

Suddenly, without warning, he grabbed his throat and began choking violently, convulsing.

"Rick, what is it?"

"It's like my throat is on fire! Something in the food! Oh, God, I've been poisoned! I'm dying! These men have killed me!"

I sat forward and raised my voice to penetrate his panic. "It's not happening now. You're just observing it, you're just watching a moment from a life a very long time ago. You're safe. You're perfectly safe. That's a whole other life, not this one, and you have nothing to be afraid of. In this life you're living now, you're never going to be poisoned, not ever again." I kept up a firm, reassuring monologue until Rick's choking subsided, his convulsions stopped and, wringing wet, he went limp on the sofa. His breathing slowed and became peaceful. He didn't bother to wipe away the tears that were streaming down his face, and I thought what a relief those tears must be.

Rick's wife, Robin, stared when he emerged from my office, and she saw that he was smiling. It was obviously his first smile in a very long time, and it lit her eyes with hope as they hugged. She called me a few weeks later to report that Rick was healthy, happy, and back at work, not a trace left of the panic that had held him captive for so long.

"Rick's psychiatrist can't believe it," she added.

"And you should have seen the look on his face when I told him Rick was cured by a psychic."

"Let me guess." I laughed, having been through this before. "The psychiatrist claims I cured Rick with nothing but a posthypnotic suggestion."

"That's exactly what he said," she told me.

"Robin, if all Rick needed was a posthypnotic suggestion, why didn't his psychiatrist give him one?"

She chuckled. "Good question. I'll pass that along."

"Better yet," I said, "tell him I'm working on a book that will explain how and why Rick was healed, and all he has to do is read it with an open mind."

To Rick's psychiatrist, and to all of you, welcome to the blessed healing power of cell memory.

THE TRUTH ABOUT PAST LIVES

I WANT YOU TO KNOW—not just believe, but *know*, to the core of your spirit where the truth lives— that you are eternal. The life you're living right now is just a tiny step in the never-ending journey of the unique, cherished soul God created for no one else but you, a step of your own design toward your own greatest potential. Your current lifetime won't end in death. It will end with your spirit simply freeing itself from your body and returning Home to the perfect higher dimension it came from called The Other Side.

The miraculous gift of eternity means that the singular essence that is you will always, always exist. I'm not talking about your turning into some philosophical, imaginary nonentity when you're through with this body. I'm promising that you will forever be the very real, living, breathing being you are now, who thinks and feels and laughs and grows and changes and learns and loves and is loved by God every moment of your endless life. And just as eternity means you will always, always exist, it also means you have always, always existed.

That's a fact. You have been alive since the beginning of time, in a gorgeous unbroken continuum, moving back and forth between earth and The Other Side many times. You have lived on earth in many different bodies, during many different eras in many different parts of the world under many different circumstances for your own carefully chosen purpose, depending on the goals and needs of your spirit's progress. Please don't let the term "past lives" mislead you into thinking you've arrived this time around as a separate person from who you've been before, alive, then dead, then alive again. No, what you're living right now is simply the current phase of one life, the same eternal life your spirit has been living and will go on living forever.

If that seems confusing, or hard to imagine, you don't have to look any further than your present lifetime to help you picture it. No matter how much or how little you consciously remember, it's safe to say that since you were born, you've been an infant weighing no more than a few pounds, unable to walk or talk or care for yourself; a toddler taking its first awkward steps and trying to learn what a toilet is used for; a five-year-old, scared or excited or confused or eager on its first day of school; a thirteen-year-old starting to experience the heightened chaos of adolescence; a twenty-year-old emerging into adulthood with more bravado than wisdom. In other words, in this one lifetime you've taken many physical forms, gone through many levels of physical and emotional maturity, and learned many lessons. Those forms and levels and lessons don't just happen and then vanish as if they never occurred. That infant, that toddler, that five- or thirteen- or twenty-year-old you used to be didn't appear and then cease to exist. No, through it all, you've always been *you*, a rare, complex, sacred work in progress unlike any other spirit ever created. At the moment you're reading this, and at the moment I'm writing it, you and I are nothing more and nothing less than the sum total of every instant we've experienced, no matter how dramatic or how trivial, and we'll keep right on changing and evolving, learning and growing with every instant we experience from this moment on.

Now take a giant step back in your mind until you can sense some inner, thrilling glimpse of the most endless, star-filled horizon you can imagine, one rush of this infinite universe you're part of. And in that step back, look at your life, with all its forms and phases, and understand that it's nothing but a smaller version of the eternal life you're living as God designed it. Whatever you've looked like in previous centuries, whatever stages of learning and growing you've struggled through, whatever lessons and changes lie ahead, they're simply strides along your path toward the most exquisite, enlightened, perfect *you* that you can be—God's beloved child with every infinite breath you take. Your past lives, here and at Home, are no different than the stages of this life, pieces of the same puzzle, parts of the same whole and, like every other moment of your past, affecting your life today in more ways than you might imagine.

MY INTRODUCTION
TO PAST LIVES

As many of you know, I was born psychic, into a
family with a three-hundred-year psychic legacy.
Unfortunately, while I was endowed by God with
more than my share of psychic gifts, I wasn't especially endowed with more than my share of spiritual
insight. I could easily see and hear spirits and ghosts,
so I never had to wonder about the existence of The
Other Side and the fact that our souls transcend
death. But when my Grandma Ada, who was my
closest friend, mentor, confidante, and inspiration,
started talking to me about past lives, I didn't disbe-
lieve her; I just frankly couldn't imagine why I
should care. For one thing, I misunderstood at first
and thought that "past lives" meant I had been several different people, which didn't make much sense
to me—what would be the earthly point of that in
the grand, cosmic scheme of things? For another
thing, if I had been a pioneer, or a French courtesan,
or even Cleopatra in a past life (I wasn't, by the
way), so what? I still had chores and homework and
a horrible mother to deal with, and more psychic
skills than I knew what to do with, no matter who
I'd been, so if there was no practical purpose to this

past-life noise, why bother learning about it? Instead, I focused my energies on handling being psychic, building a relationship with my sometimes bothersome Spirit Guide, Francine, pushing my luck with the nuns at the Catholic school I attended, and trying unsuccessfully to just fit in and be "normal," whatever that is.

I've written at length in my books *The Other Side and Back* and *Life on The Other Side* about my college years, studying religion, English literature, and psychology toward my passionate interest in becoming a teacher. I also described the intensive hypnosis courses I found so fascinating that I became a certified master hypnotherapist and began using hypnosis during psychic readings. In those same books I discussed the client who came to me about a weight problem and, under hypnosis, began telling me in the present tense about building pyramids and then lapsed into such a long stream of nonsense syllables that I thought I was witnessing a full-blown psychotic meltdown. Curious to a fault, I sent a tape of that session to a professor friend at Stanford for his objective opinion, and I was shocked when he called three days later to inform me that those "nonsense syllables" were really a fluent monologue in an ancient Assyrian dialect perfectly appropriate to the pyramid builders in Egypt many centuries ago.

Grandma Ada had talked to me extensively about past lives. Francine, my Spirit Guide, had talked to me extensively about past lives. Spiritually, philosophically, and psychically, I already knew that our souls are eternal, which is certainly consistent with the idea of past lives. But not until that gray afternoon twenty-five years ago, when I saw that shy, plainspoken man spontaneously relive a life in seventh century B.C., did I become passionate about the subject of reincarnation and committed to exhaustively researching it. I read everything about it that I could get my hands on, and studied with hypnotherapists experienced in the area of past-life regressions, determined to never again just sit there saying "huh?" if and when a client took the opportunity of hypnosis to travel back to another time. I learned to safely guide my clients into the immense wealth buried in their own history, while making sure that one hundred percent of the information revealed came from them, not from me. And to my amazement, I quickly discovered that the information they unearthed was both fascinating and incredibly accurate.

By then I had assembled and trained a small, tireless staff of coworkers, which I formalized into the Nirvana Foundation of Psychic Research. One thing I wanted to establish from the beginning of our exploration into past-life regressions was whether or not any of those past lives were valid. If my clients were using our sessions to spill out a stream of colorful detailed fantasies, that was fine with me. But I wasn't about to jeopardize my credibility by reporting fairy tales as fact to my colleagues in the psychic, psychiatric, and medical communities. It quickly became my hard-and-fast rule that I wouldn't document or report any past life a client returned to unless we were able to meticulously verify that that life had actually taken place. It wasn't easy—this was many years before computers and the Internet came along—but we dived exhaustively into public records throughout the country and at the amazing San Bruno Archives in northern California. When a hypnosis subject described a life as Margaret Dougherty in Boston in 1801, with three children and a husband who was a cobbler, we dismissed it as fiction until and unless we were able to prove that a woman named Margaret Dougherty had indeed lived with her cobbler husband and three children in Boston in 1801. Time and time and time again, verifiable past lives spilled out of one client after another, my files on them grew into the hundreds, and I was convinced beyond any doubt that we have all lived on this earth many times before and have clear memories of those lives hidden for safekeeping in our subconscious minds, just waiting to be released.

Through documented past-life regressions, I had proof that our spirits never, ever die, which was more than rewarding enough to satisfy me. I had no idea that I'd only scratched the surface of the importance of past lives. In fact, even when I began witnessing the miracles those past lives unlocked, it took Francine, from her front row seat on The Other Side, to explain to me what was happening.

THE MIRACLE OF PAST LIVES

So there I was, feeling hilariously self-satisfied by the sheer volume of confirmed past-life regressions in my files and their validation of our souls' eternity, when a client named Henry walked stiffly into my office wearing a neck brace. He'd been suffering from chronic pains and spasms in his neck since his early thirties, he explained, and he'd spent thousands of dollars to hear from one doctor after another that there was absolutely nothing wrong with him. He had actually come to my office for a reading about a possible career change, but with his permission I put him under hypnosis for some much needed relaxation and relief before the reading started. Before I knew it, he was telling me about his life in France in 1790, where, as a young widower with nothing to lose, he became a notoriously daring, zealous soldier in the French Revolution until he was executed at the guillotine at the age of thirty-three. We were both especially moved by his realization that the wife he'd loved and lost in that life more than two centuries ago was the same woman he was happily married to in this life, which explained why the two of them "somehow" knew from the moment they met that they belonged together.

Three weeks later I spoke at a charity benefit, and the first person to greet me when I came offstage was Henry, looking a thousand percent healthier and more comfortable without his neck brace. It seems his pain had noticeably diminished the day after he saw me, and on the fourth day he felt so completely cured for the first time in years that he and his wife had ceremoniously burned the neck brace in their fireplace. He was amazed. I was amazed. The only one of us who wasn't amazed was Francine, my Spirit Guide, who I'm sure was watching all this with a long sigh, wondering how obvious something had to be before I'd be bright enough to put two and two together and come up with four.

If you've already pieced this together, you're miles ahead of where I was at the time. Chronic neck pain, starting in Henry's early thirties. Doctor after doctor saying there was nothing wrong. A previous life that ended with death by guillotine at age thirty-three. And once we uncovered it, the pain went away. Duh.

Francine's policy with me has always been, "I can't give you the answers unless you ask the questions." It's harder than you might think to come up with all the right questions. But this experience with Henry finally prompted me to ask her one night, "I love proving to my clients that there's no such thing as death, but is there more to be gained from past-life regressions than I'm getting?" Her one-word answer changed the course of my research, the direction of my work, and the lives of countless clients from that moment on.

That one-word answer was "Healing."

I was so exhilarated by the idea that there was healing to be found in past lives that I didn't stop to wonder how it worked or why it worked, I just wanted to prove to myself *that* it worked. Francine had never lied to me, and she still hasn't, but as she knows better than anyone else, I'm an absolute, unapologetic skeptic. I've never taken her word, or anybody's word, for anything. I have to experience things firsthand and test them over and over and over again before I'm convinced. And healing through past lives was no exception.

Since the very beginning of my psychic and spiritual work, I've enjoyed very close, stimulating relationships with members of the medical and psychiatric communities, sharing ideas, mutually referring clients and exchanging theories and research results. Several of these colleagues had been exploring the subject of reincarnation right along with me, and it was shortly after this revelation from Francine that we scheduled a weekend-long seminar about the truth or fiction of past lives and the soul's survival. I decided it would be as good a time as any to try a past-life healing regression on a random volunteer from the audience—no setup, no rehearsal, no script, and certainly no prearranged "ringer" (*ever!*) to fake the experience, just me and a total stranger giving healing regression a spontaneous try. The rest of the panel was less than enthusiastic, the gist of their concern being "What if it doesn't work?"

I shrugged. "Then, it won't work. But we'll never know if we don't try, will we?"

The auditorium was packed that weekend. I have to admit, even though my colleagues and I had all been friends for years, I felt a little outgunned as we made our entrance onstage and I scanned the row of nameplates in front of our chairs, which as far as I was concerned read "M.D., Ph.D., M.D., Ph.D., Ph.D., M.D., and some psychic woman." But nothing loosens me up more quickly than a microphone and a crowd that's open-minded enough to at least show up.

I perversely chose the least enthusiastic of the volunteers for the demonstration, an attractive, successful-looking man who introduced himself as Neil, a mortgage broker from a suburb of Houston. I briefly explained to him and to the audience what to expect during the hypnosis process, and then, just before we started, I asked him offhandedly if there were any physical or emotional problems he'd like to address while he was "under." He talked about a recurring pain in his right foot that had never been properly diagnosed or treated, and a private fear that even people who claimed to love him complained behind his back about what an inadequate disappointment he was—the last fear you would have expected from a man who outwardly seemed to have everything going for him.

Neil was bright, responsive, and refreshingly honest, exactly the kind of subject I enjoy because it was so obvious that he'd tell the truth, even if the truth were that nothing was happening and he considered my pitiful regression efforts to be a colossal waste of time. I relaxed him into a hypnotic state and gently guided him back through this life, his death in a previous life, and then into the heart of that life itself. Suddenly he almost seemed to shrink into himself. His right foot twisted and turned under and in. His voice became thin, apologetic, sad, and barely audible. His name was Calvin, he told me. He was twelve years old, living on a farm in Virginia, and the year was 1821. He was born with a clubbed right foot, which made him a shameful burden to his parents, who'd had their hearts set on a strong healthy son to help work the fields. His schoolmates relentlessly made fun of him or ignored him completely, and his only friends were his family's menagerie of animals, none of whom seemed to think there was anything wrong with him at all; they just loved him unconditionally. By the time I eased Neil back to the present, there wasn't a dry eye in the house.

Then, thanks to Francine, before I "woke" him, I added for the first time, *"And whatever pain or fear or negativity you might have carried over from a past life, release it and let it be resolved in the white light of the Holy Spirit."*

His posture straightened, his foot returned to normal, and he offered a preoccupied "thank you" as he stood and left the stage. He was obviously moved by his visit to one of his previous lives, as were all of us who witnessed it. Several weeks later he called to report that the pain in his foot had never reappeared, and that he'd slowly but surely stopped even wondering, let alone worrying about, what his loved ones said about him behind his back.

After the demonstration, my colleagues asked a question that I've been asked a thousand times in the years since: "How do we know this alleged 'past life' isn't just a fantasy the mind comes up with to relieve pain?" It's a fair question. I asked it myself when I first started doing regressions. But if these past lives were simply a survival technique the mind dreams up, why did I have file cabinets full of detailed proof that the "fantasy" lives were very real? And why would my clients "fantasize" past lives that were so invariably mundane?

The answer I keep coming back to most often, though, is "Who cares, as long as it helps?" If a purple-spotted giraffe can offer reliable healing, I'll ride into the room on a purple-spotted giraffe. The fact that past-life regressions heal is enough for me, and for the thousands of clients whose lives have been freed from long-buried, undeserved burdens.

I was ready to make a lifelong commitment to the healing power of regression. First, though, I finally needed to find out how and why it held such miracles.

CELL MEMORY: THE LINK BETWEEN PAST AND PRESENT

BIOLOGY WAS NEVER what you'd call a real passion of mine during my school years. So when Francine informed me that the key to healing regressions was something called "cell memory," I braced myself for something too complicated for me to understand and/or too boring for me to sit through. Wrong again. Knowing that I respond best to the simplest possible logic, she presented cell memory to me in a series of step-by-step basics:

- Our bodies are made up of billions of inter- acting cells.

- Each of those cells is a living, breathing, think- ing, feeling organism, receiving, retaining, and reacting very literally to the information it receives from the subconscious mind. Un- der hypnosis, for example, when the subcon- scious mind is in charge, if we're told that a hypnotist's finger is actually a lit match and that finger touches our arm, the cells of our

arm will form a blister, exactly as they're pro-
grammed to do when they're burned.

- It's in the subconscious that our spirit minds
  live, safe, sound, and always intact, no matter
  how healthy or unhealthy our conscious minds
  might be.

- Our spirit minds remember every moment our
  souls have experienced, in this life and every
  other life we've lived since we were created.

- The instant our spirit minds enter our physical
  bodies, they infuse the cells of our bodies with
  all the information and memories they possess,
  and our cells respond accordingly until our
  spirits leave our bodies again and head Home.

- Our cells react in very real, literal ways to the
  memories from this life and previous ones that
  our spirit minds infuse them with, whether
  our conscious minds are aware of those memories or not.

- And so by accessing those *cell memories*, we can
  rid ourselves of long-buried illness, phobias,
  pain, and trauma, and also re-create the greatest emotional and physical health our spirits
  have ever enjoyed.

Cell memory, then, is all the knowledge our billions of cells contain and act on, instilled by the spirit minds that inhabit them in passing, as our spirits make their way through the eternity God promised us from the moment of our creation.

I promise you've experienced a minor version of cell memory, possibly without thinking much about it at the time. A sudden whiff of flowers or cologne or fresh-baked bread, an unexpected song on the radio, the sight of a porch swing or a child's quilt or a Christmas tree; any number of sensory images can blur the present with the past, sending you back with such a flood of familiarity that you don't just remember that past time with startling clarity, you feel a rush of every emotion you felt then, as if it were happening all over again. That same tangible, total rush of familiarity is exactly what our spirits experience when they find themselves in a human body again, after years or decades or centuries in the limitless, gravity-free perfection of The Other Side. The lines between past and present blur as every cell of the body is inundated with the reality of other times and places when our spirits occupied other human bodies and, alive and sentient as they are, our cells begin responding to anything and everything they perceive to be the truth.

So Neil, for example, my audience volunteer, had demonstrated cell memory in action before I even understood what it was. Based on the information Neil's cells received from his spirit, all the painful, unresolved events of a whole other life as a boy named Calvin were real, present, and still valid to the cells of the body he was occupying now, and still causing him real, present, valid physical, and emotional pain. But as soon as his spirit mind found its way to that "thorn" in its past, so that the thorn could be removed, he was finally able to heal.

And in case I still doubted the power of cell memory, it was shortly after Francine had begun teaching me about it that I "coincidentally" (yeah, right) met two people who made it an inarguable fact. The first was Julie, a woman in her early fifties. A doctor friend of mine had just performed a successful kidney transplant on her, and it seems that Julie, who had never smoked or touched alcohol in her life, awoke from surgery with an intense craving for a cigarette and a martini—two passions of her kidney donor, it turned out, that I was able to rid her desire for by convincing her new cells through hypnosis that those cravings weren't relevant to this new body they were housed in.

The second was much more dramatic, with a much happier ending than I could ever have orchestrated or made up. Molly, age ten, had received a heart transplant from a seventeen-year-old stabbing victim named David. It was months after David's murder, when the police had few clues and no suspects in custody, that Molly began having nightmares about a dark figure in a ski mask lying in wait for her with a knife. Through hypnosis, Molly was able to separate from her fear, remove the dark figure's ski mask, and identify the face of a young man named Martin—not a face or a name she knew, but, it turned out, a longtime acquaintance of David's. The police were notified, and Martin was brought in for questioning and ultimately confessed to the murder, all thanks to cell memory and its intimate interaction with the truth our spirits hold.

By now I felt about cell memory the way I'm told a lot of people feel about their computers: the more I learned, the more there was to learn and the more I wanted to know. And as it turned out, I had only scratched the surface.

BIRTHMARKS

A GOOD FRIEND OF MINE, a neurologist who shared my addiction to research, asked me one day to participate in a study he was conducting about a possi-

ble link between birthmarks and congenital illnesses. He was convinced that birthmarks weren't
just random quirks of skin pigmentation, and he was
hoping that I could take a poll among my steady
stream of clients and, between my psychic readings
and past-life regressions, see if I noticed any birth-
mark/health connection.

Birthmarks weren't something I'd sat up nights
wondering about, but it was a small favor for a friend
to ask. If he turned out to be right, it might lead to
some fascinating medical diagnostic possibilities. To
be honest, though, I doubted it, and I know I sounded
more enthusiastic than I felt when I answered, "Sure,
I'd love to, count me in."

I apologize for repeating stories from previous
books, but a first is a first, and a client named Billy
was definitely my first when it came to studying
birthmarks. He'd come to me for a regression in the
hope of finding out who in his present life he might
have known before. We had no luck with that. In fact,
the only past life he was interested in discussing was
his twenty-two years as an American Indian in the
early 1800s, a life that ended in battle when he bled
to death from a knife wound to his right leg, a couple
of inches below the knee. It was a brave, exciting, and
tragic life, and I was so involved in the story that I almost forgot to ask him before he left my office

whether or not he happened to have any birthmarks. He did. Just one. A purplish discoloration, like an angry unhealed wound, about two inches below his right knee. I still remember how self-conscious I made the poor man when I gaped at that birthmark a little too long and a little too incredulously—he had no memory of what was said during his regression, so he had no way of knowing that I was simply shocked to see what looked exactly like a scar from an almost two-hundred-year-old stabbing, in the precise place on his leg where he was mortally stabbed.

I wrote it off as just a very odd fluke, jotted it down after the session ended, and added a note for my neurologist friend that Billy had no illnesses, congenital or otherwise, for his birthmark to be connected to. I was certainly intrigued, though, and curious enough not to drop the subject. I was careful from then on never to mention birthmarks until after regressions, to make sure my clients didn't try to second-guess why I was asking and reach for an explanation. And as the next week, the next month, then the next six months progressed, I found not one correlation between birthmarks and illness, but a *ninety-percent correlation* between birthmarks and a serious or fatal injury from a past life.

There was the college professor with a long, slender reddish shadow across his mid-thigh, whose life in sixteenth-century China ended when he bled to death from a leg amputation. A retired seamstress had a diamond-shaped discoloration on her left shoulder, exactly where an arrow had pierced her when she was a Sioux Indian warrior in the mid-1800s. A horse trainer revealed a past life as an accused Salem witch for which she was hanged, and at the end of the reading she showed me a six-inch white birthmark across her throat. A policeman had a quarter-inch-wide strip on the back of his head where, since birth, no hair had ever grown, which "just happened" to correspond to the spot where a jealous lover had buried a hatchet in his skull in turn-of-the-century Egypt. A recording artist whose right ankle bore a dark, angry slash regressed to a nightmarish life in England in 1789 in which his hands and feet were tied to a bed for months at a time in an asylum.

The stories in my files go on and on and on, numbering well into the hundreds. Again, if only half or two-thirds of my clients had demonstrated a connection between their birthmarks and their past lives, I honestly wouldn't have considered the subject of birthmarks so remarkably fascinating. But ninety percent was too overwhelming to ignore, especially when it was so consistent with my other cell-memory research. The conclusion was obvious: the spirit enters the body with crystal-clear memories of the traumas and major injuries it experienced in previous bodies, and infuses the cells with those memories. The cells, in response, form physical evidence of those past injuries, like scar tissue from a whole other lifetime.

You may be wondering about the ten percent of clients who didn't show a birthmark/past-life connection. Those were the clients who didn't happen to have any birthmarks at all, and there seemed to be a pattern to that as well. It wasn't that they hadn't experienced any past lives. It was that the severe traumas their bodies went through in past lives were resolved in that lifetime. If, for example, you were hanged in a past life for stealing a horse but you were truly innocent, that issue was unresolved and you might easily bear traces of the hanging in the form of a birthmark, while if you were hanged for stealing a horse you actually stole, there was resolution, the subject was closed when that lifetime ended and you won't retain any residual marks. If you were the innocent victim of a catastrophic fire, you're very likely to have a past-life scar from being burned, but if you died in a fire you deliberately started, there won't be a birthmark because that life ended with no unfinished business.

So again, if you don't happen to have a birthmark,

congratulate yourself on having put some past-life issues behind you. If you do have one, don't obsess
about the past-life issue it implies that hasn't resolved
itself yet. Instead, every time you look at your birthmark from now on, take a moment to appreciate that
you're getting a glimpse of your own sacred eternity.

MORPHIC RESONANCE

I HAD BEEN deeply involved in studying cell
memory for a couple of years, learning more about
it every day thanks to Francine, my own research,
and the always incredible openness and generosity
of my clients, when a lovely man named Mark came
in for a reading. In the course of our conversation,
out of nowhere, he began telling me about his recent trip to England. I quickly recognized a familiar
look and tone as he talked that I run across a lot, an
interesting combination of eagerness and reluctance, so I gave him the sincere reassurance I knew
he needed: "You can say anything you want to me,
Mark. With my life, you think I'm going to call *you*
crazy?"

He laughed, took a relieved breath, and let his

story spill out of him in a rush of words he'd obviously been saving up for weeks. "I'd wanted to visit London all my life," he said, "although I had no idea why. No one I knew had ever been there, and I hadn't even read that much about it. Anyway, my first day there I signed up for a tour of the city. We were only a few minutes into it when the oddest feeling came over me that this place I'd never been before felt familiar, almost like home, like I somehow belonged there. I kept reminding myself how impossible that was, but before long I couldn't ignore the fact that I actually knew where I was. We'd turn a corner, and I'd know we were on our way to St. Paul's Cathedral, or that we'd be passing a park on our right and there would be a building on our left with two stone lions guarding its entrance. I'd think, 'And now we're in Chelsea,' and 'We're coming up on Scotland Yard,' several seconds before the tour guide announced it over the loudspeaker. This kind of thing went on for the whole two weeks I was there, especially the day I rented a car and drove to a small house in the countryside fifty miles north of London that I swear used to be a pub I had a sense of being homesick for, and the words 'my favorite pub is gone' went through my head. I couldn't resist asking about it in the nearby town, and sure enough, the house had been converted from a pub about three generations earlier. I've been shaken up about this ever since I got back, but I haven't told anyone. I was afraid they wouldn't believe me, and I wouldn't blame them. Can you please tell me how a thing like that could happen? Am I psychic, or insane, or both?"

The answer is, Mark was neither psychic nor insane. Instead, he'd experienced a perfect example of a relative of cell memory called "morphic resonance," which Francine describes as a case of *déjà vu*, multiplied by about a trillion. Morphic resonance occurs when the spirit mind is confronted with a place, or a person, that's so profoundly familiar from a previous incarnation that it experiences almost total recall and infuses the conscious mind with a flood of recognition. Mark's conscious mind had no way of knowing this city it had never visited before, but his spirit mind held cherished memories of not one but two happy lifetimes there, and of that little pub in the northern countryside he'd owned in one of those lifetimes, no differently than you or I might remember a beloved childhood home or a dear friend from our school years. Thanks to morphic resonance, those memories were so powerful that they became part of his mental and emotional consciousness—he didn't just know his way around, he felt a sense of belonging, and a sense of being home, that he could neither understand nor deny.

I'd been studying cell memory and morphic resonance for several years, and channeling Francine's
lectures on those subjects, when I went to Kenya for
the first time. It was there that I learned that talking
about morphic resonance is nothing compared to actually experiencing it. Like Mark with London, I'd always had an odd yearning to visit Kenya without ever
questioning why, and I was as excited as a child at
Disneyland when I stepped off the plane in the
Kenyan capital of Nairobi. The more I saw of the
country, the more I fell in love with it and knew I'd
be back many times (thirteen so far, to be exact). But
full-blown morphic resonance didn't really set in and
overwhelm me until I arrived in Mombasa, the colorful, bustling seaport on the coast of the Indian
Ocean. I was welcomed by a group of scholars and
archaeologists who'd been living in and around
Mombasa for years, and they were graciously taking
me on a detailed tour when I blurted out, "Wait,
don't tell me any more about this city, let me tell
you." And with complete confidence, I began giving
directions to and pointing out major attractions, I
even told them on several occasions what used to
be located on a site where something entirely different sat now. I knew Mombasa, Kenya, as if I grew
up there, and in my spirit mind, I clearly did. I heard
one of the men whisper to another, "I told you she's

psychic." Being psychic had nothing to do with it. It was just the same morphic resonance, the same re-sounding echoes of the past from our eternal souls, that all of us will hear and feel and know in this life-time if we'll simply pay attention and never, ever push it away.

It's true. Whether or not you ever experience morphic resonance about a place, I can virtually guarantee you'll experience it about a person, or persons, sooner or later. Just as you can know a strange city on sight as well as you know your home-town, you can find yourself knowing a stranger within moments as well as you know someone you've grown up with, like meeting for what logic tells you is the first time while your souls exchange an imme-diate torrent of silent, subtle, subconscious memo-ries. I'm not talking about that myth called a "soul mate," or even the kindred souls we find along the way from The Other Side. I'm talking about those people who immediately inspire you to think, "Well, look who's here," and their physical features, their sex, what name they're calling themselves, or what they do for a living are completely beside the point. You don't need me to tell you who they are in your life. I promise you, if you'll scan your family, friends, coworkers, and even your enemies with an open mind and ask yourself the simple question, "Have I known this person before?" you'll be able to answer with a quick, easy yes or no to each and every one of them. Then think back to the moment when that seemingly impossible familiarity rang as the truth in your spirit, and you'll understand exactly what morphic resonance is and, more important, feel the miracle of looking into another's eyes and recognizing proof of the infinite survival of your own soul.

CELL MEMORY AND READINGS

HER NAME WAS CATHY. She was in her mid-thirties, beautiful, smart, a very successful career woman, happily married with two gorgeous children. She'd asked for a reading to help her through her mother's death a year earlier, which she was still having a terrible time dealing with. The ongoing depth of her grief confused her, because she and her mother had never been especially close, nor had they even liked each other very much. Our talk of grief led to talk of loss, which led to talk of her palpable fear of loss, and before long we got to the core of that fear of loss, which she'd simply projected onto the event of losing her mother: she was terrified of losing her husband, not to another woman, but to his premature death.

Logically, it didn't make much sense. Her husband Nick was in excellent health, took great care of himself, and had no family history of serious illness. Cathy and Nick had met through a mutual friend when they were both sixteen years old, and she remembered taking that first look at him and thinking, There's the man I'm going to marry. Eight years to the day later, he proved her right. Theirs was a happy, healthy, very secure marriage. But instead of relaxing and appreciating it, Cathy lived under this oppressive dark cloud of panic about outliving Nick, to the point where she was essentially grieving his death decades ahead of time. Outliving him was such a strong reality to her that she could only come up with one possible explanation—it had to be a premonition.

Luckily, there was another explanation: Cathy was in the grip of deeply imbedded cell memories from not one, but two past lives, which I knew even without the benefit of regressing her. Just as my psychic gifts allow me to read life charts for this incarnation, they allow me access to charts from past lives as well. So I was able to explain to her that this was her and Nick's third lifetime together, mutually charted that way for the happiness that eluded them twice before.

It wasn't just wishful thinking that made Cathy so sure on sight that Nick was the man she'd marry. She recognized him from her chart and from those other incarnations in which he'd been tragically taken away from her when their lives together were just getting started. As far as her cell memory was concerned, Nick always died on her too soon when she was occupying a human body, so it was understandable that she was braced for him to do it again.

Usually a regression is more thorough and efficient than a reading when it comes to getting rid of a problem that's rooted in cell memory. Let's face it, it's always more effective to experience something than to just hear about it. It speaks volumes about how ready Cathy was to let go of her fear and put it behind her that this reading resolved it for her without her needing a regression. It also speaks volumes about the accuracy of my analysis of Cathy and Nick's past lives together, for which all the credit goes to God, not to me. It's a fact, carved in granite, that while our conscious minds can be fooled, often with hilarious ease, our spirit minds are infallible when it comes to telling the difference between the truth and a lie. If I had made up some colorful fictional fairy tale about Cathy and Nick's previous incarnations for her entertainment, she might still have enjoyed the reading, but afterward she would have been just as fearful of losing him as she was when she walked into my office. Believe me, I haven't worked this hard for the last forty-eight years to have my clients wake up a day or a week or a month after seeing me and discover that our time together did them no good at all. And that's exactly what would happen if my past-life readings and regressions consisted of anything less than the truth, because truth is the only thing that makes a lasting impression on our souls.

CELL MEMORY
AND THE DARK SIDE

THE FACT THAT I CAN READ CHARTS for past lifetimes as well as for this one has led many people, including friends in the psychiatric community, to ask if I can trace the previous lives of the evil among us, those destructive, often well-disguised sociopaths I categorize as the Dark Side, to see if maybe a "cure" to their behavior lies hidden in their spirits' history.

I've written at length in *The Other Side and Back* and in *Life on The Other Side* about the Dark Side. Dark entities are those who have chosen to turn away from God and devote their energy to destroying His light anywhere and everywhere they find it. They're remorseless, manipulative, often charming and charismatic, and completely without conscience. Sadly, they don't segregate themselves from the rest of the society, nor do they make themselves easy to recognize. Some dark entities destroy by committing actual murders, like Adolf Hitler, Charles Manson, Ted Bundy, and Jim Jones. But others go through life quietly destroying such spiritual essentials as faith, self-respect, hope, love, trust, and peace of mind. They can be our parents, our children, our coworkers, our spouses or lovers, our politicians, our movie stars, our athletic heroes, even our supposed best friends. They seduce those of us who love God and all His children into trying to rescue them, preying on our compassion and belief in the basic goodness of humankind to draw us close enough to disarm. They're the reason I've said so often that the spirits and ghosts around us don't frighten me in the least; it's the human residents of the Dark Side we need protection from.

Again, by their own choice, dark entities don't go to the sacred joy of Home when they die. Instead, they go through a hollow, bottomless, Godless void called the Left Door and then right back to earth in utero again, in a continuous horseshoe cycle that can go on for centuries, until they're caught in mid-cycle by watchful, concerned rescuers from The Other Side and embraced into the healing purity of God's eternal light.

Without the benefit of paradise between lives, the Dark Side recycles into the womb again with none of the Spirit Guides and Angels who accompany most of us on our trips away from Home, and with no life chart to guarantee the spiritual progress the rest of us design for ourselves. If they did have life charts for each of their incarnations, those charts would consist of nothing but the simple game plan: "Do as much spiritual, emotional, psychological, or physical damage as possible."

And that's why, sometimes to my frustration, I can't begin to read the past-life charts of dark entities: they *have* no charts, for the lives they're living now or the lives they lived before. In a way, it could be fascinating, and probably valuable, to be able to know who Charles Manson or Saddam Hussein used to be, or who among the current dark entities on earth was once Hitler or Jack the Ripper or Jim Jones. In the very early days of my career, I used to wonder what on earth I would do if and when a dark entity sat down in my office wanting a reading or a past-life regression. I've come to realize that that will never happen. Dark entities aren't curious about their progress toward spiritual perfection, although they might be gifted at talking about it if they think it will seduce their audience. They don't worry about their relationship with God or with the rest of humankind, and they certainly don't concern themselves with whether or not they're accomplishing the goals of a chart they never wrote to begin with. They can't be tracked back in time like the rest of us, and they can't track themselves. Not only would it be impossible to regress them, but also they couldn't possibly care less.

So if, while you're reading this, you're getting nervous and wondering if you might be a resident of the Dark Side whose past lives amount to nothing but a continuous cycle of abuse and destruction, here's your answer: the simple act of wondering means you care, and genuine caring is something the Dark Side would never, ever do.

THE MEDICAL COMMUNITY

SINCE THE BEGINNING of my career I've enjoyed healthy, mutually respectful relationships with the medical and psychiatric communities. Even those doctors who are skeptical about psychics have known after a few conversations that I'm not some slick, flaky rip-off artist, cleaning out people's wallets with empty promises, that instead I share their genuine, passionate determination to leave my clients better than I found them. I've referred a lot of clients to them, and they've referred a lot of clients to me. And they know they can always trust me to make something very clear to everyone I come in contact with: *No psychic, including me, should ever be considered a substitute for a qualified medical or psychiatric professional.*

When I started talking about cell memory to my physician friends, it's safe to say I wasn't exactly greeted with a loud chorus of "Cell memory! Of course! That makes perfect sense!" In fact, if I hadn't already established some credibility with them through my readings over the years, I'm sure they would have laughed, hung up in my ear, or both. Being a skeptic myself, I didn't blame them for having trouble believing that a lot of physical and psychological problems are rooted in unresolved past-life experiences. But they agreed with my bottom line that if it works, it's worth a try. Besides, my cell-memory work is risk-free, and I never accept payment from medical and psychiatric referrals, so there was every-thing to gain and nothing to lose for all concerned.

As always, the referrals were extreme by defini-tion, those cases in which my doctor friends had run out of options and weren't seeing any results. The first call came from a surgeon at a veterans' hospital regarding a patient named Royce. Royce had suffered a devastating back injury and been through more than a dozen operations that should have started him on the road to recovery. Instead, he was in such con-stant, excruciating pain that for weeks he'd been beg-ging his doctors to sever his spinal cord—even total paralysis sounded more bearable to him than tolerat-ing that pain for one more minute. But the surgeon who called me was understandably desperate to ex-plore every possible less drastic alternative, even if it meant entertaining such goofy, improbable concepts as "psychic" and "cell memory."

My heart ached for Royce from the moment I walked into his hospital room and saw him lying there, his eyes dull from having suffered too much for too long, his once-handsome face gray and haunted. He still had the grace to offer a quiet "Thank you for coming" when I explained who I was and that I was there to help him if I could. He was in such urgent need for relief that he gave in to hypnosis with sur-prising ease, considering his misery.

A half hour later Royce was telling me about his happy life as a man named Thomas in a small Georgia town in 1855. His voice was relaxed, with an easy drawl, as he described his wife and four sons, and his hard, rewarding work on the farmland they shared with his parents. He was proud that his whole family attended church together each and every Sunday, rain or shine, and his youngest son could recite the Lord's Prayer by heart by the time he was four years old. The spring Thomas turned thirty-eight, he was painting his parents' house when the ladder collapsed and he fell two stories and broke his back. He lay paralyzed from the chest down for almost three months before he died. A broken back ultimately killed him. Related cell-memory number one.

And then it was 1721, in Spain. Royce was now Paolo, eighteen years old, the privileged son of nobility. His great passion in life was a beautiful twenty-two-year-old woman named Cristina, who was unfortunately married to his older brother. One night when Paolo was on his way home from a clandestine visit with Cristina, his brother ambushed him and plunged an ax deep into his back, killing him instantly. Related cell-memory number two.

I prayed for Royce to release those devastating past-life wounds into the white light of the Holy Spirit so that his body could focus solely on its pain in this life and not cling to its cell-memory belief that back injuries are inevitably excruciating and fatal. He was exhausted but peacefully preoccupied when I brought him out from under hypnosis, and he managed a weak smile when he murmured, "No wonder I feel like someone buried a knife in my back." He was already asleep when I slipped quietly out of the room.

Three weeks later, Royce's surgeon called with an update. After my visit Royce had never again asked that his spine be severed. In fact, he'd started to show a remarkable recovery, had insisted on getting out of bed for the first time in months, and was already taking some proud, tentative, elated steps with the help of a walker. The surgeon ended the conversation with something I've heard since my cell-memory research started and still hear to this day: "I don't know what you did or how you did it, but it worked." And I said the same thing to him that I'm still saying to this day: "It's not me, it's God and the people I regress. All I do is clear the path for their spirit minds to enter those places they've been yearning to find their way back to."

Around that same time, through a psychotherapist I'd known since my college years, I met Talia, a professional athlete. She'd suffered a concussion while preparing to try out for the summer Olympics, and

she'd been unable to speak from the moment she re-
gained consciousness. Doctors had run countless
tests and found no medical reason for her silence. After weeks of working with her, a team of psychiatrists
had ruled out all the possible mental and emotional
causes they could think of. My psychotherapist friend
apologized for letting it slip that calling me was his
"last resort," but I've heard that a million times before, and it never has offended me. I'd rather be a last
resort than no resort at all if someone needs help.

Talia was in her late teens, a natural beauty in incredible physical condition, as confused as her doctors at the loss of her voice and understandably
frightened by it. By now she was able to communicate in short sentences through a handheld voice box
she carried with her, and she laughed when I warned
her not to complain too much about it—it made the
two of us sound almost identical.

The first past life Talia revisited was a happy, un-
eventful one in Japan that held no cell-memory clues
to her current condition at all. But she was clearly reluctant to move on to her next life during her regression, and it took some time to convince her to stay in
what I call the "observant position," to just watch the
events that were upsetting her without actually reliving them. Finally not one but two more past lives
spilled out, both of them moving her to tears as she

described them to me. In the first, she was a young girl in ancient Syria, running in terror as an earthquake roared through the marketplace while she and her mother were shopping. A falling pillar crashed into her head from behind, pinning her facedown on the ground, and her last desperate cries for help before she died were too muffled in a pool of her own blood for anyone to hear.

Next came a fascinating life in Egypt. She was sixteen, prized and revered by many and feared by some as a priestess and a powerful seer. One night, despite a battery of guards hired by her father, three kidnappers made their way into her room while she slept, hit her on the head to knock her out, stole her away to a cave and, during the time they held her for ransom, cut out her tongue, believing she would have no power if she was unable to speak. Their torture of her continued until she bled to death, at which time they abandoned her body and were never captured.

Two past lives in which a blow to the head was immediately followed by an inability to speak or be heard, and now, at almost exactly the same age she'd been when she suffered fatal injuries in those lives, she suffered a concussion in this life and found herself unable to speak for reasons no one could diagnose. It was either another case of cell memory in action or, as a lot of skeptics would insist, Talia's mind was hard at work making up stories in an effort to recover from a trauma. All I know or care is that fifteen years later a woman rushed up to me backstage during a television appearance I was doing and beamed. "Hi, Sylvia! Remember me?" I wish this weren't true, but facts are facts—almost without exception, the answer to that question is likely to be "No." I'm not great with names and faces to begin with. Add to that thousands upon thousands of clients in the last forty-eight years; lectures, book signings, and television and radio appearances in more cities all over the world than I can count; and consultations with literally hundreds of doctors, law enforcement officers, and private investigators, and I promise you, I'm almost guaranteed to be completely stumped when someone surprises me out of nowhere with "Remember me?" But I'm much better with readings and regressions that make a big impression on me, so when the woman added, "I'm not using a voice box anymore," I knew exactly who she was.

I was thrilled to hear that Talia fully recovered after our session together, but I was disappointed to hear that it had taken six months. I expect quicker results than that, and I never blame the client when it doesn't happen—I blame myself. I don't believe in handing out little hints of help and relief over a long period of time, to keep a client coming back for reading after reading and handing over check after check. Occasionally, with an extremely distressed client or an especially complicated series of problems, I'll do a follow-up reading or regression, but never more than two. Many of my ministers have become very capable, well-trained regression hypnotists, and I've given them strict orders that if it ever takes more than one or two sessions to make a significant difference in whatever issues their clients are struggling with, I need to know about it and they need more training before I'll let them continue with that particular area of their work.

At any rate, one thing you can always count on, for better or worse, is word of mouth. It's how I built a clientele in the first place. So it came as no surprise when all these years later, it created a whole new surge of calls asking for help through past-life regressions, whether the doctors, psychiatrists, and clients who were calling cared about or believed in the validity of cell memory or not. It never bothered me, and it never will, that the vast majority of referrals are cases that doctors and psychiatrists had given up on. I love being tested. I love a good challenge. And most of all, I love making a difference.

PSYCHOSOMATIC
MALADIES

THERE ARE FEW THINGS more frustrating than describing a pain or an illness to your doctor and being told that the problem is "all in your head." Actually, it's been my experience that that's almost true. Pains and illnesses that don't necessarily show up in blood tests and X rays and MRIs and CAT scans, that are usually referred to as psychosomatic, *are* in your head—in the subconscious, where the spirit mind lives and where cell memory gets its information.

Don't misunderstand, I have all the respect in the world for most medical and psychiatric doctors, but I do wish they would eliminate the word "psychosomatic" from their vocabulary, because the implication of it is "There's not really anything wrong with you, you just think there is." I truly can't imagine a client sitting down in my office and describing a problem that's important to them and my responding, "Nonsense, that's not a problem, you just think it is." If you tell me something's a problem for you, I believe you. And if I can't help you solve that problem, you'll *never* hear me say, "Oh, well, then, it must not be real." It's my responsibility to find the right solution and/or lead you to someone who can, and we should all demand the same from every doctor we see.

I can't begin to estimate the number of referrals doctors have sent me with a description of the client's complaint and then an added comment that "I'm guessing it's psychosomatic." Add to that the clients who have come to me on their own after their doctors gave up on them for "psychosomatic" conditions, and I'm sure the total is well into the thousands. What also totals well into the thousands is the number of "psychosomatic" conditions I've personally cured, simply by releasing the cell memory that's really causing the condition in the first place.

Elise was a classic example. She came to me on her thirtieth birthday about a frightening physical problem she'd been having since she was fifteen years old—on an average of three or four times a week, with no warning and no pattern to make it predictable, her throat seemed to close up on her so that she had to gasp for air until it relaxed again, which might take anywhere from a few minutes to almost an hour. It was impossible to count the number of times she'd been rushed to emergency rooms for shots that would relax her windpipe enough to allow her to breathe and swallow normally again. She even had several friends on standby, who knew that if they got a phone call with nothing but a gasping sound and the phone being frantically pounded against the wall on the other end, they were to alert 911 to send an ambulance to Elise's apartment. Fifteen years later Elise had been through every test that eight different doctors could think to put her through, and to six different psychiatrists, none of whom could find any physical or psychological reason for these scary, potentially fatal spasms. Their conclusion: the condition was psychosomatic. Translation: we give up.

Some regression subjects like to visit several different past lives while they're "under," from the sheer freedom and novelty of the experience. Not Elise. She instantly jumped to a primitive, long-ago life in Africa. She had no idea what her age was or what year it was, because the small tribe she was part of didn't bother with numbers to mark the passage of time. She only knew that she was in her early child-bearing years, which probably meant her mid-teens, and that she was tall, slender but strong from hard work in the fields around her village. Her skin was a beautiful ebony, and her short black hair was secured beneath a bright turbanlike twist of mud cloth, which is a hand-loomed fabric dyed by applying native soils. She had walked by herself to a stream some distance from the village to retrieve a jug of water, when she sensed movement behind her and heard a low, feral roar. She turned to see a lion that had crept up on her and was now just a few yards away, poised to attack. She didn't even have time to be frightened or call out before the huge cat was on her, taking her down and, as jungle cats do for a quick kill of their prey, tearing out her throat with its powerful, razor-sharp jaws. She was dead almost instantly and still remembered being separate from her body and watching with some fascination as the lion dragged it away.

I didn't need to point out the connection between this past-life death from a mortal wound to Elise's throat and the present-life chronic tightening of that exact same area that cut off her air and her ability to swallow. Elise pointed it out to me the instant she "woke up" from hypnosis. She said she felt "liberated," and her sense of relief was obvious as we prayed for God to help her release that long-buried trauma from the cells that were holding the memory of it and let it be absorbed into the white light of the Holy Spirit.

Over the next month after her regression, Elise's throat closed again twice. Both times it relaxed and reopened in a very few minutes on its own, with no need for medical attention. After those two episodes, and in the year and a half since I saw her, it has never happened again.

It's worth emphasizing that in Elise's case, as in so many other cases of problems caused by cell memory, the condition started at the same age in this life that the trauma occurred in the past life. She wasn't able to specify fifteen years old in her past life in Africa, but "early childbearing years" is certainly close enough for comfort to the age in her present lifetime when she suffered her first episode. If it somehow makes more sense to you to write all this off as "coincidence," feel free, although you have to admit it's fairly uncanny as coincidences go. If cell memory is as logical to you as it is to me, though, it's simply the spirit mind remembering that when it's occupying a human body, something very dramatic happens to that body's throat during its mid-teen years.

There's not a psychic in the world, including me, who's one hundred percent accurate. But my success rate at giving significant relief to people whose physical or emotional problems have been dismissed as psychosomatic is well over ninety-five percent. Is that because I'm smarter, or wiser, or more skilled, or more compassionate and well-meaning than the doctors and psychotherapists who were unable to help those people? Absolutely not. Could it be because they haven't yet tried solving their patients' undiagnosed complaints through cell memory? It does seem like a possibility, doesn't it?

HYPOCHONDRIA

I'D BEEN DEEPLY INVOLVED in cell-memory studies for almost two years, writing about it and lecturing on it, and excitedly discussing it with my curious but skeptical colleagues, when a call came from an internist I'd known and enjoyed since we sat on a healing panel discussion together a year earlier. I knew I was being respectfully teased when he kicked off the conversation with "Have I got a referral for you."

I chuckled and reached for my notepad. "OK, Doctor B., let's hear it."

"Her name is Lorraine. She's sixty-one, she's been a patient of mine for fifteen years, and she's as healthy as a horse."

"Then, what's her complaint?"

"You name it. Any disease she reads about in the papers or hears about on TV, she's convinced she's got it and insists I run urgent tests to prove it. Nothing irritates her more than finding out all the tests came back normal and there's not a damned thing wrong with her. Instead of appreciating her good health, she spends her life constantly braced for some dire medical catastrophe."

"In other words," I said, sighing, "you're sending me a hypochondriac."

"Exactly. She's a sweet woman, Sylvia, but she's driving herself and me crazy, and I thought maybe . . ."

"You thought maybe she could drive me crazy for a while, since I'm already halfway there anyway with all this cell-memory nonsense," I suggested, not entirely kidding.

He laughed. "You said it. I didn't. But, hey, if you think it's too tough a challenge for you to handle, forget I called."

As if I'd fall for such an obvious, childish dare.

Lorraine was in my office and under hypnosis six hours later. Several of my colleagues had warned me against wasting my time. "Don't beat your head against a wall," they said. "One thing you can count on with most hypochondriacs is that they aren't about to give up the attention they get from all their imaginary diseases."

I knew what they meant, of course. I've run into the same kind of thing occasionally with clients who begged me to get rid of a curse someone had put on them that they were convinced was ruining their lives. You've never seen such defiant resentment as when I explain that they don't need me to get rid of a curse, because *curses don't exist*. It's as if by taking away the possibility of a curse, I'd threatened to take away a valued part of their identity. And when I refused to accept their money because they were asking me for a service I couldn't perform in good faith, they invariably stalked out in a huff. Amazing.

But I owed it to Lorraine to give her the benefit of the doubt and assume that her presence in my office meant she sincerely wanted help. Dr. B. was right, she was a sweet woman, and when she listed her current symptoms and illnesses she was sure she'd had, despite all evidence to the contrary, she seemed more genuinely confused by them than attached to them. She went "under" without the slightest reluctance.

She started her regression slowly, but within minutes words and past lives were pouring out of her like some massive emotional dam had burst. The lives themselves were remarkably unremarkable, one after another after another. What quickly became fascinating was the stunning variety of ways those lives had ended. In her many times on earth, Lorraine had died of breast cancer, leprosy, consumption (an old term for tuberculosis), pneumonia, Asiatic cholera, a ruptured appendix, toxemia, jaundice—and those were only the lives we covered in our first two and a half hours together.

Now, obviously, for every life we live on earth, we're going to die of something sooner or later. But what I found with Lorraine, and with the many other hypochondriacs I've worked with since, is a long unbroken succession of very slow, painful deaths, none

of the sudden or peaceful passings most of us experience a majority of the time when we're ready to head
Home again. So when the spirit mind enters another
new body, it infuses the cells with memories that in-
volve suffering, a variety of diseases, and a general
message that the human body is a flawed, uncomfort-
able, unhealthy place to be. It's no different than if, in
this lifetime, you lived in a series of apartments, and
in every apartment you found yourself facing one
major problem after another, from leaky plumbing to
no heat to repeated break-ins to bug infestations to
faulty wiring to impossibly noisy neighbors. After
enough bad apartment experiences, you could move
into the safest, quietest, most impeccably maintained
apartment in the world and not be able to enjoy it because your history has led you to the understandable
conclusion that if you're in an apartment, something's bound to be wrong, whether whatever's
wrong with it has shown up yet or not. That's exactly
what the spirit mind of a hypochondriac experiences
when it returns to a body, and it immediately starts
sending those "brace yourself" memories and messages to the cells, which react by waving red flags
at the slightest hint that, sure enough, this body's as
big a mess as all the others have been. There's not a
traditional medical or psychological test that can de-
tect ailments that have their roots in cell memory, so

doctor after doctor, psychiatrist after psychiatrist will swear that the only thing wrong with a hypochondriac is their need for attention. The truth is, what's wrong with a hypochondriac is that their cells haven't released the past-life memories that keep them on such stressful alert and haven't yet learned that the human body really can be a perfectly safe and comfortable place to live.

Lorraine was one of the rare clients who needed two regression sessions to sort through all the lives and catastrophic illnesses she'd experienced. But when she'd finally brought them all out into the light—i.e., when all the thorns from her previous incarnations had been exposed and removed so the wounds from them could begin to heal—her hypochondria vanished. She recognized and appreciated how healthy this current body of hers really was, she started taking great care of herself, she still saw Dr. B., but only for annual checkups, and she's still thriving today at eighty years of age.

I need to emphasize again that cell memory is not the cause of all our physical and psychological problems, and that no one values the medical and psychiatric communities more than I do. I know, though, with absolute certainty, that there's no more powerful supplement to a responsible health regimen than releasing the past-life negativity cell memory contains.

Also I would love for every doctor, psychiatrist, and psychologist to give it a try with their patients, if only to prove me wrong, and then write or call my office with their results. Again, I really don't care how goofy it sounds or how goofy you think I am for suggesting it. The bottom line is, cell memory works. It heals. So please, with all due respect, just *don't knock it till you've tried it.*

POINTS OF ENTRY AND THE OTHER SIDE

NOT ALL PAST-LIFE regressions and cell memories are negative. Far from it. Those memories also include the happiness, joy, and love we've experienced on earth and, best of all, our glorious lives on The Other Side. Specific memories of Home aren't as easy to access as our memories on earth, for the simple reason that if we remembered The Other Side too clearly, we'd be even more chagrined about being here than we already are. But ninety-nine times out of every hundred, when I take a client through their death in a past life, the next thing they describe without any guidance from me is being embraced into the brilliant, holy, unspeakably beautiful light of God and their arrival into the most exquisite place they've ever seen.

By the way, one recent notable exception to that experience proved how determined the spirit mind really is to grab an opportunity to be healed, not to mention how a client's spirit mind takes charge during a regression and I'm just along for the ride. His name was Alain, and he came to me for help with what he described as a "sheer terror" of being alone. Everything in his life, from his and his wife's six children to his career as a tour coordinator, was designed to keep him surrounded with people, but inevitably there would be brief hours from time to time when he was by himself and he would find himself in tears, overwhelmed by a sense of dread and a feeling that somehow even this momentary isolation was a punishment of some kind for some wrong he couldn't identify, let alone atone for.

The first past life Alain revisited was a happy one. He was in Egypt, in a busy, highly prestigious position within what he called the Royal Guard, and one of his primary responsibilities was to entertain visiting foreign dignitaries. He and his wife and their ten children lived with his parents and several other relatives in a large house full of love and laughter. He lived well into his sixties and died from a very sudden heart attack.

He described his quick, painless death casually, understanding it perfectly as just another event in a much larger life that will never end. He talked briefly about how wonderful it felt to be rid of that silly gravity-bound body, and then, as I always do at that point, I asked him to tell me what he saw next. He said he was in a green field: a valley with beautiful mountains all around him, and animals.

I nodded, smiling to myself at how predictable it is for clients to experience a few moments on The Other Side after an especially happy life, and asked, "And how do you feel?" with my pen poised above my notepad ready to jot down his equally predictable answer, some version of "ecstatic," or "euphoric," or "joyful." I almost gave myself whiplash doing a double take when instead he answered, "Desolate."

I tried to keep the surprise out of my voice. "Where are you?"

"Peru," he said.

No disrespect intended to Peru, but it's not paradise. My silent expectations were completely beside the point. He'd already leapt to another life. "What are you doing in Peru?" I asked.

He began sobbing so hard that he couldn't get words to come. I repeated over and over again, "Go to the observant position, Alain. What you're seeing and feeling isn't happening now, it's all in the past, in another life, we're getting rid of it so it can't ever hurt you again. Separate yourself from it. Observe it. Just watch it and tell me what you see." After a few minutes he calmed down, although a few tears continued to escape from his tightly closed eyes.

His life in Peru, it seems, was the result of a self-imposed exile. His wife and infant son had died in a fire in their home, a fire set by his enraged mistress when he'd ended their relationship. Alain wasn't there when the house burned. He had gone to a nearby town to drown his self-pity in a friend's bar and passed out for the night. He returned to a nightmare the next day—his wife and son were dead, his house was reduced to charred rubble, and his mistress had killed herself. And as far as he was concerned he was one hundred percent responsible for all of it. The thought of trying to rebuild his life never entered his mind. He didn't feel entitled to a life anymore, or another moment of happiness. So he left, without a single good-bye to his remaining family and friends, deliberately depriving himself of everyone and everything he knew and loved, and disappeared to the mountains, taking a job tending sheep in exchange for a place to sleep, silent and solitary, until he died from exposure twelve years later.

No wonder the poor man associated being alone with being punished, and what an awful burden for him to carry until his spirit mind was finally given a chance to release it that day in my office. Again, though, while he threw me for a moment with his trip to Peru when I was poised to hear about The Other Side, he also helped illustrate how our souls yearn for healing. Until they heal, our cell memories will continue to react as if the wounds are as real, current, and painful as if they've just now been inflicted.

That experience with Alain made me wish there was a quicker, more efficient way to help my clients get directly to the life or lives or events that are causing them cell-memory problems, without their having to wade through past lives that may not be relevant to what's bothering them. All past lives are interesting, if only to prove to a client that there's no such thing as death, that we really are eternal. But when there's a specific issue a client is struggling with and hurting from, why not get right to where it came from instead of wandering around for a while and leading up to it? My Spirit Guide, Francine, assured me it was very simple: all I had to do was direct the client to go to what she called the "point of entry," which is simply the moment at which the event or events happened that created the cell memory to begin with. In Alain's case, for example, the point of entry was the discovery that his wife, son, and mistress were dead because of actions he set in motion. Lorraine's points of entry were all those slow, lingering deaths that led her to be constantly on alert for yet another fatal illness. Every cell memory has a point of entry, and it turns out that on hearing that phrase, the spirit mind, in its desire to be healed, will move to it immediately during a regression. Since Alain, the ministers I've trained as hypnotists have found the same thing I have: when a client wants to tackle a specific, especially painful issue that's rooted in a past life, the quickest way to uncover it is to ask for the point of entry; and every single time, the "thorn" that's hurting them will be revealed in the very next story from the very next life they describe.

Points of entry and memories of The Other Side combined with gorgeous, moving clarity during a recent regression with a woman named Gloria. Her husband of thirty-eight years, Martin, had died suddenly a month earlier. They'd had one of those rare, magical marriages in which they were as deeply in love on the day he died as they were when they were high school sweethearts. She was in that indescribable abyss of grief that only comes when we lose someone who has become part of the essence of our soul, so that we never quite feel whole again in this lifetime without them. I remember hugging her the minute she stepped through my door and thinking, "There's grief, and then there's *this*."

Gloria's appointment was for a reading, but I decided a regression might be more helpful. I knew we'd find that she and Martin had spent many lifetimes together, and it could reassure her that they would absolutely be together again. She accepted the offer, and considering the thick dark veil of grief we had to penetrate, she "went under" fairly easily. Revisiting random past lives was not what Gloria needed to get to the heart of the searing emotional pain she was in, so the first thing I said to her was, "Gloria, I want you to go to the point of entry."

Not one client has ever asked what that means. As I said, the spirit mind seems to understand it perfectly. And Gloria was no exception. She immediately described a life in northern Europe in 1721 and another in Italy in the mid-1800s. In both lives she and Martin were deeply in love. She was his wife in northern Europe and his mistress in Italy. The first point of entry she went to happened in 1721, when she was at his bedside, inconsolable, as he died and left her alone, thousands of miles from the family she'd left behind to devote her life to him. In 1850, the second point of entry, she died in his arms after giving birth to the only child they ever had together.

And now, with his death in this life, they'd been separated again. Small wonder her grief was so horribly deep. Thanks to cell memory, she was mourning being torn away from him for the third time.

I knew her pain would be eased slightly by this chance to release those past-life heartaches into God's hands through the white light of the Holy Spirit, but I decided to try something more, something I'd never tried with a client before. Since our spirit minds carry cherished memories of The Other Side, and I knew Martin had made a safe, joyful trip Home, I wanted to see if I could reunite their spirits for a few moments. Through this, she could get comfort and reassurance from the one person she needed the most. So while Gloria was still under hypnosis, I took her through the tunnel we've all traveled through so many times before and then stepped back to let her move past the light on her own, make herself at Home, and describe what was happening. As you know if you've seen me or other mediums at work, spirits don't always show up on demand, and I was careful not to promise or even mention Martin in case they didn't find each other.

I watched her face relax and soften into a contented smile. I asked her what she was seeing.

"I'm in a garden," she told me. "I can't begin to describe how beautiful it is. It's as if even the colors are alive. I would say I've never seen anything like it, but somehow it seems familiar. I'm walking along a stone path, and I know my way around. And there's a white marble building in the distance, so white it's almost sparkling."

If you read my book *Life on The Other Side*, you'll recognize, as I did, a perfect description of the Gardens of the Hall of Justice. All I said was, "Keep walking as long as you like, Gloria."

She let out a short, sudden gasp.

"What is it?" I asked.

She whispered in awe, "Martin."

Good. He'd found her. I asked her how he looked.

"Wonderful," she said. "Happy. Healthy. Younger."

That figured, since everyone on The Other Side is thirty years old, but I wasn't about to interrupt to point that out.

There was a long, peaceful silence. Finally Gloria quietly announced, "He's gone."

A few minutes later she was fully awake and sitting up on my couch, clearly preoccupied and moved by the experience she'd just had. "It's funny," she told me, "I told him how much I love him and miss him, and he assured me he's with me all the time. But I don't think either one of us said a word out loud." Telepathic conversation. A very common way for spirits to communicate. "He held me before he left. I could feel his arms around me. This may sound crazy, but I'm sure I even smelled the aftershave he always wore."

"It might sound crazy to your friends when you tell them about it, but trust me, it doesn't sound crazy to me," I said.

"I honestly don't care what my friends think, or what anyone else thinks, for that matter. There's not a doubt in my mind that what just happened was real and that I just saw my husband alive and well." She stood and moved to hug me. "I'll never forget this, and I can't thank you enough."

The thanks weren't mine to accept. They belonged to God, and to Gloria's own spirit and cell memories of The Other Side, which made the trip there so easy and familiar an experience for her. Like I said, it was the first time I'd ever used regression as a route to reuniting a client with a deceased loved one, and it won't be·the last. Gloria called a month later to report that while she was still grieving and missing Martin's physical presence terribly, just knowing with absolute certainty that he was with her, watching over her, and waiting for her had renewed enough of her hope and strength to get herself showered, dressed, and back to work again, which was light-years ahead of the numb emotional paralysis she'd been going through since the day he died. And let's face it, if you've ever experienced grief, you know how much courage those baby steps back toward normalcy really take.

It was yet another example of the healing potential of cell memory, and like Gloria, I'll never forget it.

In the upcoming sections of this book I'll be sharing just a handful of the thousands of documented regressions my ministers and I have had the privilege of witnessing since the beginning of my work with cell memory. In addition to being fascinating, these past-life experiences illustrate far better than I ever could how eternal our lives really are and what a rich, vast wealth of knowledge and memories we carry with us into each new lifetime.

But these stories are more than illustrations. Somewhere in them, you'll find a fear or a chronic physical malady or some other problem you or a loved one can identify with all too well. Beyond that, you'll find the path someone followed into their own cell memories, to the source of that same problem, so that they could release it into the purity of God's white light and, by healing past wounds, create a healthier, more peaceful future.

PART TWO

Phobias and Other Emotional Obstacles

Liza

• *The Fear of Abandonment*
• *The Need for a Family*

L IZA WAS THIRTY-SIX. She'd been married to Clint for four years and was, as she put it, "desperately" in love with him. "Desperate" in her case meant that she constantly found herself trying too hard to please him, not because she was afraid he'd hurt her but because she lived with a nagging feeling that there was something temporary about their marriage, and that she was constantly in danger of disappointing him and his leaving her as a result.

Out of her love for Clint and her belief that it would help cement their bond, Liza had started trying to have a child by him almost from the moment they started dating. When she was unable to conceive after a year, she began going to doctor after doctor after doctor, who put her through procedure after procedure after procedure, and she was now living with the awful irony that her extreme efforts to get pregnant had made it an impossibility. Clint couldn't have been more reassuring and supportive, but she was convinced he was just putting up a front, and that underneath it, he resented her for being such a failure. She feared he would inevitably move on to a better, more satisfying, more deserving woman who could offer him the family she couldn't.

The first life Liza regressed to was in eastern Europe. She was a peasant, and Clint was a soldier in a red uniform with black boots. They were in love, deeply committed to each other, and secretly planning to marry behind the back of her cruel, strict, overly possessive father. But the same night they had planned to run off together, her father figured out what was happening and literally dragged her out of the house and eventually to a distant convent, where she lived the rest of her short life as a virtual prisoner, bitter and alone, never seeing Clint again and never knowing what if anything he was told about her sudden disappearance.

Next she was in a newly settled colony in what is now Delaware, where she and her husband (who in that life she didn't believe was Clint) had arrived just weeks earlier, bravely but reluctantly leaving their families behind in England for the thrilling promise of fresh dreams in the New World. Liza was pregnant with their first child, and they were excited about starting what they hoped would be a large family. But in her sixth month of pregnancy, her husband was killed in an accident on the fishing boat he worked on. In the grief and stress Liza went through after his death, she lost her baby. So there she was, a young, childless widow, seemingly a million miles away from her family and friends, and she was dead herself in less than a year from what she described as a broken heart.

Then came a life in Egypt. Liza was a devoted companion and lady-in-waiting to a powerful woman she felt was a member of royalty. The great love of her life was the woman's even more powerful brother, who was already committed to a loveless but politically expedient betrothal. The two of them kept their passion a secret for several months until they were caught together. Liza was immediately sent away by a small group of men she recognized as similar to our presidential Cabinet, charged with being a threat to a marriage these men considered imperative to the future of the country. When she was allowed to come back several months later, her lover was married and gone, the powerful woman she worked for was now cold and abusive toward her for what the woman felt was a calculated betrayal, and she was treated as an outcast and even a potential traitor for the remainder of her lonely life.

No wonder Liza's cell memories were all about abandonment and her intense desire for a family. At least three times, she'd been unfairly torn away from the men she'd intended to spend her life with, denied even the comfort a child could have given her, and taught that the inevitable outcomes of love were isolation and an earthly future of nothing but numb emotional emptiness. So from the moment she fell in love with Clint, every cell in her body began sending out the messages her spirit mind had infused them with from past experience: brace yourself for an unhappy ending, and if you want a child, act fast or be prepared to spend the rest of your life alone.

Liza left my office fascinated but not convinced that the past-life experiences she'd seen so clearly weren't just products of her vivid imagination. Her conscious mind was also afraid to indulge in the luxury of feeling secure in her marriage to Clint. But she promised to make a nightly habit, for one month, of praying that any pain and negativity she'd brought over from past lives be released from her cell memory and her spirit mind into the white light of the Holy Spirit, so that she could truly appreciate all she had to give and receive in this life. As I told her, "I don't care if you think it's the dumbest idea you've ever heard, just humor me and do it. And if you don't notice any difference in your life after a month, call and tell me I don't know what I'm talking about."

It was actually Clint who called, six weeks later. "Whatever you did to my wife, you should bottle it," he said when I picked up the phone. "She used to make up excuses to call me three or four times a day at work just to make sure I was really there, she'd grill me every time I left the house about where I was going and when I was coming back, and she'd freak out if I was even a few minutes late. Frankly, she was starting to feel more like a warden than a wife, no matter how much I reassured her that I wasn't going to disappear on her. But she's done a complete turn-around since she saw you. She's more relaxed, she's more confident, she's much happier, and best of all, she finally seems to trust me. I look forward to coming home these days instead of dreading it like I used to, and I just wanted you to know how much we both appreciate it."

An even better postscript arrived a year later, when I got a beaming Christmas photo of Liza, Clint, and their newly adopted baby daughter. And no, by the way, they didn't name her Sylvia.

Cynthia

• A Self-Destructive Need for Attention

CYNTHIA WAS THIRTY, a referral from a psychiatrist friend. Her need for attention was obvious even before she entered my office. I could hear
her talking and laughing in the reception area at
about twice the volume anyone would consider normal, and because of her habit of gesturing wildly
when she talked, she managed to knock over a lamp
and spill her coffee while simply introducing herself
to my staff. When I walked out to retrieve her, I
found that her too tight, too short, low-cut dress,
over-teased hair, and extreme makeup were all calculated to scream the same message as her booming
voice and exaggerated gestures: "Look at me!"

At first she seemed determined to convince me
that she was one of the happiest clients I'd ever met
and that she'd agreed to see me not because she had a

problem but because she'd seen me on television and thought it would be fun. As for this "need-for-attention" thing her psychiatrist kept complaining about, it was a silly overreaction on his part. After all, who doesn't love attention, and what on earth was wrong with it, if it made her happy? Sure, a lot of people seemed to dislike her for it, but anyone could see they were just jealous.

I didn't have to be psychic to recognize after several minutes of this rapid-fire monologue that she was protesting far too much, and trying to convince herself as much as she was trying to convince me that she was a happy, carefree woman who loved her life. A half hour later she was in tears, her voice quiet and almost timid, as she let me behind her facade to see how lonely, sad, and out of control she privately knew she was. This need-for-attention thing she supposedly loved had cost her several jobs, where she was accused of being either too disruptive or "inappropriate." It had also led her to be compulsively promiscuous, often with her girlfriends' boyfriends, with the result that she was inevitably rejected by both before long. As for boyfriends of her own, they seemed to stay around just long enough to use her sexually and financially before moving on to women who demanded the respect Cynthia didn't, or felt she couldn't because she didn't respect herself. She was spending too much time socializing in bars, which was leading to a potentially serious drinking problem, and it was that problem that led her into therapy, as if she thought everything else was going well. But after eight months, neither she nor her psychiatrist felt they were making progress, nor did anything in her safe, secure, remarkably loving middle-class childhood hold any obvious clues about her uncontrollable, increasingly dangerous terror of not being noticed.

She was a great hypnosis subject: open, responsive, and articulate. Because her problem was so specific and pressing, I told her to go to the point of entry. She jumped straight to her sudden, violent death as a seventeen-year-old boy during a battle in the French and Indian Wars. Next thing she knew, she was alone in an endless expanse of deep green rolling hills, near a large simple stone house with a thatched roof. As I had with Alain in the reading I described earlier, I assumed at first that I was hearing about Cynthia's first moments on The Other Side. But the longer she talked, the more convinced I was that wherever she'd gone after that particular death, it wasn't Home.

There were a lot of children in and around the house, with several women in long dark dresses watching over them. Cynthia was watching them through a window and had the feeling that in order to accomplish that, she must have been able to float slightly above ground level. She desperately wanted to join the children and play with them, but she knew she couldn't. She also knew that while she could see and hear these people perfectly, they weren't able to see and hear her, as if she didn't even exist. And most of all, she knew she'd been there for a very long time, that she was somehow trapped there. What she wanted more than anything was to leave, to put an end to the overwhelming isolation she felt, standing outside that window, lost, alone, and doomed to this mute, invisible nothingness while no one around her noticed or cared.

In other words, the cell memory that was driving Cynthia's frantic desperation for attention was the horrible, helpless time she spent between lives as an earthbound, or ghost, trapped between earth and The Other Side but part of neither, "haunting" a Catholic orphanage in the Irish countryside. I can count on less than one hand the number of clients, out of thousands and thousands, who have regressed to their awful existence as a ghost, waiting for someone from Home to rescue them or for someone on earth to set them free. And in every case, those clients were struggling in their own way in this life to deal with their feeling of being an outsider, trying to find a way to be noticed, included, and embraced, which in the end was all Cynthia wanted.

As I said earlier, many times, the conscious mind can be fooled, but the spirit mind and cell memory will only resonate and respond to what it knows to be the truth. There wasn't a shred of doubt in Cynthia's mind that she hadn't imagined that earthbound non-life during her regression. She'd remembered something as real as her getting dressed that morning and driving to my office, and she felt the release of all that cell-memory pain as surely as if a long-endured fever had finally broken.

I got a wonderful ten-page letter from her eight months later. With the help of a twelve-step program and a real determination to make something worthwhile of her life, she was no longer drinking. Besides, she didn't have time to waste her nights in bars anymore—she'd entered college, determined to become a teacher. "I guess I still want attention from all those children," she told me, "but now I'd rather get it by helping them and being an example of someone who's made every mistake they'll ever think of and still came out okay." She was taking a break from dating until she was sure she was "healthy enough to attract a healthy relationship," and she was also in the process of making amends to the friends she'd betrayed in the past.

Last but not least, she enclosed a photograph of a lovely, fresh-faced young woman, a natural, understated beauty who was bound to attract all the attention she wanted with the peace of mind and quiet confidence she projected. I would have bet it was the younger sister of that frantic woman I'd met in my office if she hadn't added a caption that read "UN-EARTHBOUND LOVE AND THANKS, CYNTHIA."

Ryan

- *Emotional Distance from a Spouse*
- *Feelings of Ambivalence About Life*

A T AGE FORTY-SEVEN, Ryan was the picture of upper-middle-class success. He had everything he'd ever thought he wanted and more, which made it even harder for him to understand his growing disinterest in life in general and his marriage in particular. His discontent was starting to threaten too many parts of his world that he knew he genuinely treasured, and the only explanation he could come up with was that he must be in the middle of a raging, self-involved midlife crisis. "I hate the idea of being a cultural cliché," he told me, "but I hate what it's doing to my wife and me even more. I love her. We've been together for twenty-six years, for God's sake. I don't want to lose her. But she feels like all I do is push her away whenever she tries to reach out to me. And the thing is, she's right. I can feel myself doing it. I hate it, I scold myself for it, and the next thing I know, I'm doing it again. I guess it's because she knows I'm not happy, she wants me to open up about what's wrong so we can work it out together, but I can't open up because I don't have a clue what's wrong. Maybe the problem is that nothing's wrong. I have nothing to complain about, so obviously *I'm* the problem. I've lost my passion, I've lost my curiosity, I've lost my joy and my sense of looking forward to life. I just feel like I've emotionally flat-lined, and I need help finding myself again."

He called it a midlife crisis. I call it a "desert period." Most of the people I know, rich or poor, married or single, hardworking or unemployed, famous or anonymous, healthy or chronically ill, have been through that emotional flat-line Ryan described. I've been through it too, and I wouldn't wish it on my worst enemy. I gave Ryan a lot of credit for summoning the energy and the effort to come see me, because when it happened to me it was all I could do to get out of bed in the morning. I'd suffered through it one day at a time until it naturally ran its course—as it seems to do with most of us sooner or later—so I was especially intrigued to see if a regression and a cell-memory release could help speed up the healing process of this sadly common, very real problem.

In the first past life Ryan encountered, he was a

woman, a bookkeeper living in the north of England. It was a life that started tragically and seemed to stay that way. She was the only child conceived in a loveless marriage. Her mother suffered a small series of strokes while giving birth to her, and her father promptly vanished rather than take on the responsibility of an unwanted baby and a sick wife he'd already grown to loathe. From the very beginning, her mother made it clear how unwanted she really was, and blamed her for the strokes and for her father leaving. She accepted that blame and spent her life supporting and being the sole caretaker for her debilitated, cruel, vindictive mother. She never married, never even entertained thoughts of friends or parties or falling in love or the rest of the world full of promise beyond the walls of her job and the small, dark, threadbare house she returned to every night. She repressed every emotion that threatened to disrupt the familiar emptiness she'd accepted as a debt to her mother she could never repay, and all those fallow unexpressed feelings finally festered into the stomach cancer that took her life.

The second past life Ryan remembered was in Wales, in the late 1800s. He was a man this time, very tall and thin, clean-shaven, with a prominent nose and "an artist's hands," long-fingered and graceful. He was a master woodworker and furniture craftsman, and traveled throughout the country to tend to his many grateful customers. He was in his early forties before he fell in love with and married a lovely young shop girl half his age. A year later she gave him a son, and he was sure he was the happiest, luckiest man who ever lived. That happiness ended suddenly and tragically when his wife and son were killed in a boating accident. Ryan was forty-eight when he found himself alone again, and even his minister, who was his most trusted friend and confidant, couldn't begin to ease his grief. He buried himself in his work again, his skill still intact but his joy in it gone, and when death came shortly after his sixty-first birthday, he welcomed it. "It was easy, a relief," he said. "I just stopped living."

So now, in his current life, Ryan, at age forty-seven, was with a wife he loved, and his cell memory was telling him to get ready to lose her and to be prepared to say good-bye to his joy right along with her. His lifetime in Wales had taught him that all real quality of life ends at forty-eight, and his lifetime in England had taught him that going emotionally numb is an effective protection against feelings that are likely to cause nothing but pain and futility. Thanks to cell memory, Ryan was already grieving in anticipation of losses he'd really suffered a hundred years earlier, and was distancing himself as a means of defense he'd learned too well a hundred years before that. Releasing those cell memories allowed him to stop reliving those lifetimes once and for all and focus on making the most of the one he's living now.

A month after his regression, Ryan called. His voice, a flat monotone when I met him, was now a rich baritone that sounded alive and interested, and he just wanted me to know that he was taking his wife on a second honeymoon in Maui later that week and, almost more important, he was really excited about it. Five years later they're still together, thriving and happier than ever, and I'll always applaud him, as I applaud all my regression clients, for having the courage to face the past in search of a richer, more meaningful future.

Betsy

• Agoraphobia (an extreme fear of open or public places)

BETSY WAS FORTY-TWO. She had been suffering from agoraphobia for more than ten years, and despite tranquilizers and a lot of hard work with three different therapists, it was getting worse. It had cost her her marriage and her lucrative job as a buyer for a major department-store chain, and was going to cost her her house if she didn't find a way to overcome it soon.

I asked her if she remembered the first time she realized she had a problem. She did, very clearly. She was headed to her first day back at work after suffering a miscarriage in the second month of her only pregnancy, and she stopped at her bank on the way. She was standing in line when she was hit by a sudden wave of panic. It was so foreign a feeling and so powerful that she thought she might faint. A cold sweat started at the nape of her neck and spread until the back of her blouse was drenched. When she reached the head of the line and started to walk in a haze toward an available teller, she froze, disoriented. The teller's window looked as if it were a thousand miles away. The quiet voices around her sounded like she was hearing them from the bottom of a deep hollow well. She turned and ran out of the bank and had no memory of how she got home. She did remember her husband's deep concern, his unsuccessful efforts to urge her back to work, and his patience slowly but surely eroding over the years as she became more and more reclusive and less and less able to contribute to their marriage, emotionally, financially, or physically. The divorce was actually at her insistence, though— she couldn't handle the added stress of seeing the disappointment and strained tolerance in his eyes, and she frankly felt relieved when he left.

Betsy's first impulse was to have me simply tell her what was causing her agoraphobia rather than to go through a regression. Like many other clients, she wasn't afraid of being hypnotized; she was afraid she'd be unable to be hypnotized. It's true that some people "go under" more deeply than others, but I've never had a client who couldn't or wouldn't "go under" at all, or find their way back to at least one past life. I could have told Betsy what created her problem, but as I said earlier, it makes much more of an impact when clients discover those significant past-life experiences themselves. She finally opted to "try" being hypnotized, and once she quit trying and just relaxed and let it happen, she was a wonderful subject. When I knew she was ready to start her journey back in time, I decided that her situation was urgent and dramatic enough to suggest that she go straight to her points of entry.

She took a long breath, then told me she was standing at a window, in a pretty dress she'd made herself. She was seventeen years old, in Mexico, and she could see by her reflection in a small oval mirror on the adobe wall of her room that she was attractive, with a mane of thick black hair, a full mouth, and a flawless brown heart-shaped face. She stopped in the middle of her description to announce, "Someone just came in."

"Who is it?" I asked.

"My father."

"How do you feel about your father?"

"I'm terrified of him. He's here to take me away."

"Take you where, Betsy?"

She gasped as she realized, "For an abortion."

She was getting upset. Her hands started to tremble slightly. "It's okay," I assured her, "it's not happening now, you're just observing and telling me about it. There's nothing to be afraid of. Whose baby is it?"

"He worked for my father. I loved him. My father found out and beat him, and he ran away. I've disgraced my family being pregnant with no husband, so I have to be punished by losing my child. My father knows a man in another town who takes care of these things."

I already knew how this story ended, but I didn't want to lead her to it, so I simply asked, "Is it safe?"

She slowly shook her head. "I died there. I bled to death." After a pause she added, "I was glad to go. My mother and grandmother were waiting for me."

A few moments later, with my suggestion that she focus on her points of entry, she was a Japanese woman living in Kyoto. She was in her thirties when she entered into an arranged marriage. Almost pathologically obedient and eager to please, she immediately devoted her life to her husband. They had one child: a son who died of pneumonia when he was four years old. In his grief, her husband withdrew, unfairly blamed her, and began spending more and more time on long trips away from her. Her parents offered no comfort, ashamed of her for not being able to keep her husband happy and at home, and she literally starved herself to death, unloved and alone and relieved to go, six years to the day after the death of her son.

It was so understandable, then, when in this life her miscarriage triggered her cell memory to equate the loss of a child with shame, rejection, isolation, and her own death. Her innocent trip to the bank, on her way to work, was her first outing since the miscarriage, and it set off a thousand alarms inside her, screaming that going on with her life was not an option, that everyone she loved would inevitably turn their back on her and punish her, and that dying would be her only refuge. She'd been in the process of creating that loveless isolation for ten years. That day in my office, she finally understood why.

The weekend after I saw her, Betsy took a three-hour flight to the East Coast to see her ex-husband for the first time in years. Not sure if he'd buy this regression idea, she hoped he'd understand her explanation for pushing him away, no matter how far-fetched. It was better than no explanation at all. As skeptical as he was, he couldn't argue with the miraculous fact of her actually venturing out in public and onto a plane, and her warm, affectionate excitement at being with him. Six months later she's back at work as a vintage clothing buyer for a select handful of antique stores, taking courses in fashion design and computer graphics, and taking turns traveling to visit her ex-husband twice a month toward a possible reconciliation. When I pointed out that she hardly sounds like a woman who's decided to let herself die young and alone, she laughed and spoke volumes with her simple reply, "Thanks anyway, Sylvia, but been there, done that."

Wendy

• *Fear of Water*

WENDY, THIRTY-ONE AND SINGLE, was raised on an island just off the coast of Washington State. Swimming, boating, and waterskiing had been a part of her life for as long as she could remember, and when she graduated from college and started her marketing career in St. Paul, Minnesota, she willingly accepted an hour's commute to work when she rented a guest house on a small beautiful lake.

Her life was happy, drama-free, and, to use her word, "ordinary" until she was twenty-nine. She went to bed one night as usual, woke up very suddenly a few hours later in a panic at the once-calming sound of the lake lapping at the dock beneath her window, hurriedly packed a suitcase, and fled to a hotel in the city, never spending another night in the guest house on the lake again. As she described it, she felt as if wa-

ter, which had always been like a familiar friend to
her, had been unmasked for the seductive, lethal
monster it really was, and if she allowed herself to go
anywhere near it, it would destroy her. The fear hit so
abruptly and so intensely, and it was so unlike the rational, well-balanced logic that was her nature, that
she found herself wondering if maybe she'd suffered
a full-blown psychotic meltdown. Her family doctor happened to be an old colleague of mine. If she
hadn't trusted him so completely, I feel safe in saying
she would never have tried to rescue her sanity by sitting down with a psychic for a past-life regression.

You've probably guessed by now that Wendy's regression revealed that she had drowned in a past life
at the age of twenty-nine. And that's exactly right. It
was 1836, and she was traveling by ferry across the
Mississippi River to marry her fiancé, when the ferry
capsized. The weight of her long skirts pulled her
underwater and kept her from being able to swim to
safety. If you've also guessed that uncovering the cell
memory of that tragedy immediately healed the
wound and allowed her to resume her love of the water again, you're right about that, too.

But Wendy's story is a great way to introduce yet
another valuable aspect of cell memory: very often,
in getting to the root of one problem, the solution to
another problem will reveal itself, so that two or

more of the spirit's wounds end up being healed at the same time.

That was definitely true in Wendy's case. She was very moved by her regression and the crystal clarity of it, and the more we talked after my prayer that she release all past-life pain and negativity into the white light of the Holy Spirit, the more she realized that we might have answered another question she'd been struggling with for many years. She had been in love twice in her life, with supportive, healthy, attractive, successful men. Both relationships had been happy ones, progressing nicely, until, in each case, the men proposed marriage. She declined both proposals, giving the men and herself vague excuses like "I'm not ready" or "Of course I love you, I'm just not sure I'm in love with you" or "I need to concentrate on my career at this point in my life." But the truth was, for reasons she'd never understood, the mere thought of getting engaged to anyone, even substantial men like these, filled her with nothing but dread and an overwhelming impulse to run away. She ended both relationships abruptly and never saw either man again. She explained away her reaction by telling herself that some "intuition" had kicked in and prevented her from making a mistake. After her regression, she wondered if maybe it wasn't intuition at all, but cell memory, reminding her that for her, engagement ends in death. Could cell memory really be responsible for her lifelong fear of serious personal commitments?

Four years later, Wendy is happily married and teaching her three-year-old twins to swim. I happen to think that's answer enough.

Nell

• The End of a Love Affair

WE'VE ALL BEEN THERE. We all know the pain of rejection from a breakup with someone we're still in love with. It's awful, it's debilitating, and the only reliable means of recovering are time and a determined willingness to get over it.

Nell was forty, smart and attractive and level-headed. She and George had been living together for five years when he left her for a twenty-five-year-old woman who was carrying his child. More than a year had passed since then, but in spite of the help of family members, her minister, antidepressants, and eight months of therapy, the wound was as fresh and paralyzing for Nell as it was the day George moved out. She still couldn't eat, couldn't sleep, and couldn't work. She was becoming dangerously thin and anemic, her pretty brown eyes were vacant and hollow, and she was humiliated to be borrowing money from her father to pay her rent. She was frightened and confused by what was happening to her. She'd been through several relationships before, even a brief impetuous marriage, and had been on both ends of the eventual breakups. But no matter how often she reminded herself that she'd recovered from this pain before and could certainly do it again, she knew this had gone on too long—she was in real trouble, and for the life of her, she couldn't understand why.

I told her to take her time and go back to as many points of entry as she could find. A few minutes later Nell was in Germany, nine years old, living with her eleven-year-old brother and their elderly aunt in a yellow wooden house. Since the death of their parents, she and her brother had become best friends. He loved her, he protected her, he comforted her at night when her dreams made her cry, he taught her to read, he built a fire in the hearth when she was cold, he made her warm food when their aunt was too ill or tired. But most of all, he promised he would take care of her all her life—and she believed him. When they were grown up and their aunt was dead, her brother went off to fight in a war. She stayed in the yellow house, working as a seamstress, and waited for him to come home. There was no word from him until many years later, when a strange woman showed up at her door. She introduced herself as Nell's brother's wife, and told her that her brother was dead. He had survived the war but died in a fall from a horse two years later. The woman accepted Nell's invitation to stay the night, but the next morning when Nell woke up, she was gone, and Nell never saw her again. She was inconsolable from that moment on, not only from the news that her beloved brother was dead but also from the news that his military service had ended without his ever coming back for her or even contacting her. Her grief and the shock of being betrayed by the one person she was sure truly loved her were too much for her to bear, and she died of congestive heart failure—in her case, a genuine broken heart—at the age of forty-four.

It's not often that I travel back in time with my clients, but this was one occasion when I was right there with Nell and saw the strange woman who came to see her. If you've ever seen me at work, you know that I don't pull any punches, and it would be a breach of my contract with God to placate a client by telling them what they want to hear when I know it's not true. So in Nell's case, when I interrupted to tell her what had really happened, I wasn't just trying to make her feel better. In short, the woman was deeply troubled, a liar, who wasn't Nell's brother's wife at all. She had fallen obsessively in love with him while he was still in the military and killed him when he rejected her. She couldn't resist finding Nell out of cruel curiosity, but she had to disappear quickly before Nell inevitably unveiled her as the impostor she was.

I've said many times earlier, and it's worth repeating now, that while the conscious mind can be fooled, the spirit mind instantly recognizes and resonates to the truth. Nell knew she had just heard the truth about that past-life tragedy, after almost two hundred years of cell memory, suffering from the loss of a man who was, all at the same time, her brother, her best friend, and the only family she had, added to the misconception that he'd abandoned and betrayed her and therefore couldn't possibly have loved her.

The words "don't you see?" are the best bridge I've found to help a client make the connection between a past trauma and a present situation. I used them now. "Don't you see," I asked Nell, "how that unresolved heartache from another time has added layers upon layers upon layers to the pain of this breakup you went through a year ago? Both situations involved men you loved, lived with, and trusted, both involved another woman, and both in one way or another involved lies and betrayal. In this life George did to you exactly what you believed until today your brother had done to you. Now that you know the truth about that past life and can heal from it, you can finally start healing from the truth about this life: that your brother in Germany deserved your love and trust, but George obviously isn't half the man your brother was."

Nell still wasn't completely convinced it would be that easy, but she did promise she would start and end every day for the next month with a prayer for the pain, grief, betrayal, and all other negativity she'd brought over from that or any other past life to be released into the sacred purity of God's love through the white light of the Holy Spirit. I knew she was off to a good start when she left a message the next morning that she'd gone home and "exorcised" her apartment of every photo of George, every note and letter he'd ever written her, and even a "hideous" (her word, not mine) piece of jewelry he'd given her that she found out later he'd bought a duplicate of for the "other woman." I got a lovely farewell letter from her after six weeks—she'd accepted a job transfer to another state, a transfer she'd turned down twice before in case George changed his mind and wanted her back. Now she didn't care. She was eager to start a new life, and no one will ever convince her that that new life would have been possible if she hadn't made peace with a past life she never knew existed.

Sheldon

- *An Exaggerated Sense of Responsibility*
- *A Need for Everything to Be in Order*
- *An Increasingly Overwhelming Fear of Death*
- *Substance Abuse*

THERE ARE SOME CLIENTS who especially touch my heart, and Sheldon was one of those clients. He was a very gifted interior designer, a gentle and emotionally generous man, quietly spiritual and that rare phenomenon known as a true innocent, as shocked by unfairness, meanness, and dishonesty in his mid-forties as he was when he was four, despite eighteen years in a career that regularly exposed him to all that and more. If something was wrong, physically or emotionally, with anyone he cared about, he considered it his steadfast responsibility to make it right again. He worked hard, he loved deeply and actively, and what might have endeared me most of all was his adoration of animals, because they were usually better company than people and made much more sense to him.

Sheldon's compulsive need to make everything fair and okay in a world where things just aren't always going to be fair and okay, no matter how hard we try, took its toll in a few significant ways that brought him to see me. For one thing, even though he was a happy optimist by nature, it was becoming harder and harder for him to enjoy a life in which the words "what's the point?" were starting to creep in a little too often. For another thing, he was developing chest pains with no medically traceable cause and, since the day he turned forty, he was becoming more and more convinced that a sudden heart attack was going to kill him. And finally, over the years he'd slowly, surely, and quietly fallen victim to substance abuse. Just as slowly, surely, and quietly he'd entered a twelve-step program, which was helping a lot, but he worried constantly about relapsing and didn't doubt for a minute that he was still vulnerable to the sheer escape into a few hours of irresponsibility that "recreational" drugs supposedly offer. (Who coined that ridiculous term, anyway? Does that mean there's also such a thing as a "recreational overdose," "recreational withdrawal," and "recreational suicide"?)

In other words, there was a lot going on with Sheldon, but he revealed it slowly. All he had really come to see me about was his "certainty" that his chest pains were forecasting a fatal heart attack, whether his doctors believed him or not. But, as so often happens with regression clients, these other issues he was struggling with began creeping to the surface, eager to be dealt with and healed.

The first life Sheldon described was in eastern Europe. He was a tailor, with a small shop near the modest house he worked hard to provide for his wife and two children. What little they had, he proudly earned with his skilled, artistic hands, and he found great comfort in the quiet, orderly predictability of his life. One night he locked up his shop and was walking home when a robber jumped out of the shadows, shot him in the chest, and stole his pocket watch and what little money he had. He did not die peacefully. Instead, he lay there in the shadows, slowly bleeding to death, wondering what his hard work, his deliberately simple and peaceful way of life, and his total commitment to the welfare of his wife and children had accomplished, if it could all end with such a quick, violent, random, wasteful act. How had he let himself become so complacent that he didn't sense danger before it was too late, or be caught so off guard by it that he couldn't even fight it off? How dare he be so careless not to have taken a more well-lighted route home, and leave his family like this with no one to take care of them? The meager savings he'd managed to set aside wouldn't last them a month. Why hadn't he worked harder, knowing he was all they had? This fine, modest, responsible forty-three-year-old man took his last breath alone, wrongly hating himself for a life he had every right to be proud of.

Dead at forty-three, from a gunshot wound to the chest, due to circumstances beyond his control. And now, in this life, Sheldon had developed chest pains and a fear of death from those chest pains when he turned forty, and was compulsively concerned about making sure everything around him was okay and under control, all thanks to cell memory he'd been carrying without knowing it. He briefly experienced two other past lives while we were together: one in Africa and one in Mongolia. In both he was the sole caretaker of either his child or his parent, with the added responsibility of "a lot of animals" in the life in Mongolia. In one of those lives he died from a spear to his chest at thirty-nine, and in the other he died of a heart attack at forty-four.

It's my responsibility to help my clients get as much value from a reading or regression as they possibly can, but there's no question that our time together can only be as useful as they allow it to be once they've left my office. I didn't doubt for a minute that Sheldon was sincere and responsible enough that he would see to it that his regression had lasting value, and he didn't let me down. Purely by "accident" (as if there are such things), he and I found ourselves together at a small dinner party four months later. We managed to sneak off for some private time so that I could find out how things were going for him, and, more specifically, whether or not he felt that exploring his past lives and cell memory those lives left behind had made a difference. In that gentle way I have, I urged him to be completely honest, to not hesitate to say so if he hadn't noticed any positive changes—I think my exact words were, "If you lie to me to be polite, I'll kill you."

The first thing he remarked on was that since our session, he had not had a single twinge of chest pain. Not one. And on the rare occasions when he even thought about his chest pains, he was able to dismiss them with a simple "Cell memory, that's all that was." I asked if the easing of his chest pains had eased his fear of death. A look of mild shock crossed his face. "I did have a fear of death, didn't I?" he asked, amazed. "I forgot all about that. I don't even remember the last time I *thought* about death." We laughed and agreed that I could take that as a yes—completely forgetting he had a fear of death certainly qualified as a sign that his fear of death had been eased.

He then told me something incredibly gratifying:

visiting his past lives had unearthed all sorts of personal issues, like opening the door of a closet where he'd just hidden anything he didn't care to deal with, and now, rather than slam that door shut again by medicating himself, he found he had the strength to tackle the mess inside that closet and the determination to put it in order so that, as he put it, "I can finally learn to enjoy being who I am." And so, to really capitalize on the work he'd done with me, he'd increased his attendance at twelve-step meetings and, in the process, seen his fear of relapsing completely vanish. He'd also found an excellent therapist, for weekly work on who he is now and who he can be, rather than being so burdened by who he once was. His compulsive need to make sure everything was all right and under control was gone, as was his feeling that if something was wrong, it was either his fault or his responsibility to fix it. A surprise he hadn't discovered until therapy was that for years he'd had a recurring nightmare that there was a threatening presence in his room, looming over his bed while he slept. He would leap out of bed and try to run, while that presence began chasing him. That presence, of course, was one of his old selves, threatening his current sense of safety and security. Since his regression, he had never had that or any other nightmare again.

"I can honestly say I'm not the same person who

came to see you four months ago," he told me. "I feel new, and calm, and healthy, and clean, and sober. I'm not sure how much of it is the regression, how much is the twelve-step program, and how much is therapy. But I am sure that that regression, and releasing my cell memories, strengthened my commitment to sobriety and let me love myself enough to find a good therapist to help make myself even better. So no, I'm not lying to you to be polite when I say that you changed my life."

No, Sheldon, *you* changed your life. I'm just honored to have been a part of it.

Sarah

- *Depression*
- *Headaches*
- *Compulsive Overeating*

SARAH, FORTY-THREE, was trapped in a cycle that challenges so many of my clients: she was compulsively overeating because she was depressed, and she was depressed because she was compulsively overeating, a catch-22 that started when she was twenty years old. There wasn't a diet regimen she hadn't tried and faithfully adhered to, a professional diet clinic or gym she hadn't dutifully attended, or a blood test she hadn't subjected herself to in an effort to see if maybe a hormonal, glandular, metabolic, or genetic imbalance might be causing a weight problem. Her doctors unanimously agreed that being overweight was dangerous to her health. She was frightened, she felt both helpless and hopeless, and she'd heard so many contradicting facts—"It's not the calories, it's the fat content" or "Fat content is deceptive, the real key is counting calories"—that she'd finally stopped listening to them at all. She was tired of false promises, tired of trying and failing, tired of the disappointment in her blind dates' eyes when she first opened the door, tired of living in a body she hated looking at, tired of constant depression and the headaches it caused, and, most of all, tired of not understanding why any of this was happening to her.

Adding to Sarah's confusion and humiliation was the fact that in every other aspect of her life, she was disciplined, fastidious about appearances, and professionally successful. She'd graduated from college with honors, her small house and her wardrobe were impeccably maintained, and she was a gifted, tireless, and highly valued registered nurse. The irony of being able to take such brilliant care of total strangers' physical problems when she couldn't conquer her own was enough in itself to make her cry herself to sleep more often than not, and it was after an especially tearful night that she walked into my office, sank down onto the sofa, and announced, "I might as well warn you, I've already been through weight-loss hypnosis before, and it didn't work. So if you're planning to give me a posthypnotic suggestion that from this day forward, lettuce will taste like pecan pie to me, you can save your breath."

I love legitimate doctors and hypnotherapists, but I hate quacks. I've met too many clients who've been victimized by them, and the damage they can do is an outrage. I moved to sit beside her and put my arm around her shoulder. "Sarah, if you don't listen to anything else I say today, I want you to listen to what I'm about to tell you and listen carefully, because I swear to you, it's the God's honest truth, okay?"

"Okay," she answered, still tentative. "What is it?"

"There's no lettuce in the world that tastes like pecan pie, and there never will be. Now, shall we get started?"

She smiled and relaxed. I returned to my chair beside the couch and began the meditation that would ease Sarah "under." Twice she stopped me, claiming to have to use the rest room. The first time I waited for the several minutes she was gone. The second time I told her to stay where she was and not worry about it, if she had an accident on my couch, I'd clean it up later. She was stalling, afraid of yet another disappointment. After all she'd been through, I didn't blame her a bit.

Before long Sarah was in India, in the early 1500s. She was a dancer, prized for her grace and her beauty. She wore a costume of red and saffron silk that brushed in soft caresses against her long, bare, golden-brown legs as she spun in rapturous freedom for a room full of wealthy men, all of whom wanted her but none of whom would ever have her. Her heart belonged to a dark, quiet older man—a man who rarely spoke or smiled and who had many secrets from a past he never spoke of that had left him wary and wounded. He loved her, and he brought her gifts from long trips that would take him away from her for months at a time; but since the day she met him when she was twenty years old, she had never looked at or thought of any other man but him. Her greatest wish was to marry him, but he never asked, never offered her any commitment at all, and she would never have dared make demands for fear that he might leave her. So she loved him quietly, obediently, and completely, cherishing their private nights together, taking joy in the feel of his eyes on her when he stood in the back of the room of wealthy men and proudly watched her dance, and silently bearing the rejection of his not wanting her quite enough. One night when she was thirty-six, she finished dancing, left the room of wealthy men, and found an older woman she'd never seen before waiting for her in the rain. Without a word, the woman raised a gun from the folds of her skirt and shot Sarah in the head, killing her instantly.

"Who was she?" I asked.

"I don't know," she said, "but I think it was about him."

I took her through her death, through the tunnel, and safely to The Other Side, where we understand everything and all our questions are answered. I asked her again. "Who was the woman who killed you?"

"My man was an assassin," she told me quietly. "He killed her husband. I was her revenge."

In that life, she was twenty when she met the man she loved, who never married her, and because of whom she was ultimately shot in the head. In this life, her weight gain began when she was twenty, after which she suffered from depression and headaches. It didn't take a rocket scientist, or a psychic, to make that connection.

As if floodgates had opened, flashes from some of Sarah's other past lives began pouring out of her. She was in Belgium, very heavy from giving birth to twelve children, the wife of a cruel man who finally beat her to death. She was in New York, the mistress of a gangster, whom she left for what turned out to be a brief affair with another man, and she spent the rest of her life in hiding, afraid of the gangster's inevitable retribution. She was in Italy, a child, living on the streets with her mother, poor and desperately hungry, constantly being stoned by the other children in their small town because she was illegitimate. She was in Germany, married to a doctor who wanted children and, because she seemed to be infertile, subjected her to a series of drugs, shots, and serums that made her obese from hormonal and glandular imbalances and eventually killed her without ever producing a child.

"Don't you see," I asked her, "how you've been using weight to insulate yourself from the rejection, disapproval, danger, and death you've learned to associate with love, relationships, and letting yourself be vulnerable?" I pointed out that she'd been unable to find safety and security in being beautiful, in being married, or in being a mother, and even her own mother in Italy either couldn't or didn't protect her from harm, from poverty, and from hunger. No amount of willpower and self-discipline Sarah could come up with was likely to send stronger messages than unresolved cell memory, telling her that her survival depended on isolating herself and keeping potential love relationships at a distance. Her past history with obesity simply offered her an easy, accessible, and familiar way to literally create that distance, in fact a visible suit of armor, and by compulsively overfeeding herself she could protect herself from the starvation her own mother had once allowed.

The immediate change I saw in Sarah that day was dramatic. The angry, defensive, almost combative woman who entered my office was sweet, lovely, vulnerable, and peaceful when she left, and when she promised to make the prayer for releasing negative cell memories an everyday habit, I knew I could believe her.

I still have the photo she sent me a year later, beaming triumphantly at the end of a charity AIDS walk, "EIGHTY POUNDS LIGHTER AND LOVING IT!" as the caption read.

LeeAnne

• *Fear of Fire*

ONE OF THE MANY FASCINATING THINGS about regressions and cell-memory work is the number of unexpected, even unasked, questions whose answers start to unfold when past lives are given a chance to surface. LeeAnne, a twenty-eight-year-old architect, was a perfect example. She'd been to several of my lectures and was very curious about her past lives, but she also hoped in the process that she could get rid of her overwhelming fear of fire. By her own admission, it was extreme. News footage of major fires made her cry and gave her nightmares. She couldn't be in the same room with a harmless fire in the fireplace, and was literally sickened by the smell of burning wood. She couldn't bring herself to strike a match, or sit quietly relaxed without breaking out in a cold sweat when someone near her struck one. In fact, it was a major act of courage and self-control to sit in a restaurant or a friend's house surrounded by lighted candles without darting around blowing them all out.

"There's not a chance that anything in this life caused this," she told me. "I've talked to my parents and everyone else in my family, and apparently even when I was a baby I would start screaming hysterically every time my dad pulled out his cigarette lighter." She paused and took a deep breath before going on. "If I tell you something I've never told another living soul, do you promise not to laugh?"

"You think *I'm* in a position to laugh at *anyone?*" I asked.

"I know exactly how crazy this sounds, but between this fire phobia and the odor of wood burning making me sick and my fascination with her while I was growing up—"

"Your fascination with who?"

She lowered her eyes, almost too embarrassed to say it. "I'm starting to wonder if maybe in a past life I might have been Joan of Arc."

To be honest, I would have loved that. I knew she'd never been Joan of Arc, but I would have loved it. I have yet to meet anyone who's the incarnation of anyone I've ever heard of. I also knew exactly what had happened to LeeAnne in a past life. But rather than influence her regression in any way, I simply replied, "Well, why don't we get started and find out?" Several minutes later, when she was fully hypnotized and completely relaxed, I told her to go to her point of entry.

Sure enough, she didn't travel back in time to France in the early 1400s. Instead, she began describing thick ropes roughly chafing her wrists and her ankles, unable to move from the pile of wooden planks and dry branches she's standing on, surrounded by a sea of onlookers, some with faces contorted with hatred but others openly weeping. The voices are loud and mean, a chant, but she can't make out the words. Helpless, in frozen, panicked disbelief, she scans the crowd, meets one pair of eyes, a man's. In the moment before he turns his eyes away, unable to look at her, she knows he put her here, and that he's sorry and wishes he weren't too weak to stop this. Four men step forward. She sees them lighting the torches they're carrying, turning the night red-orange and crackling with anger. She's terrified, long awful minutes away from death, refusing to make a sound, refusing to give these people the satisfaction of her terror in face of the unspeakable unfairness that's ending her life.

"Go to the observant position, LeeAnne," I insisted. "This isn't happening now, you're a safe distance away, you're only watching, you're not in any danger, just tell me what you're seeing, but don't feel it." Then, already knowing the answer, I quietly said, "Tell me where you are."

"My God," she whispered, "it's Salem."

Later, after the regression, we sat talking about the experience. She knew it was real and right, and she knew it had already done the worst damage it could ever do to her over three hundred years ago, so there was no need to be frightened of it anymore. Suddenly a thought hit her. "You know what I just realized?" she asked, amazed. "I've never had any legal problems, I don't have a lawyer, I don't even *know* a lawyer. I've never been inside a courthouse before, let alone a court*room*. But for as long as I can remember, I've thought of the whole justice system as one big, corrupt, not-very-funny joke. I guess being tried, convicted, and burned to death for being a witch could have left me with a bad taste in my mouth, huh? This cell-memory idea could really make a lot of things fall into place."

Julia

• The Wrong Mr. Right

SPEAKING OF CELL MEMORY making a lot of things fall into place, a past-life regression may have saved Julia's life, or at least saved her years and years of needless pain.

Julia met Max at a friend's wedding. She was nineteen, happy, bright, and busy with art school. He was twenty, handsome, ambitious, charming, and already a rising star at a well-known stock brokerage. She remembered standing with the other bridesmaids during the ceremony, their backs to the congregation, and getting the feeling that someone was staring at her. She snuck a glance over her shoulder and met the penetrating gaze of a man she'd never seen before, and in that instant her life changed. Julia and Max danced every dance together at the reception. A month after that they moved in together, and eight months after

that they eloped to Hawaii. They were sure they'd experienced love at first sight, they were convinced they
were "soul mates," and there wasn't a doubt in her
mind that they'd spent many lifetimes together. What
other possible explanation could there be for the immediate recognition and intimacy between them, and
their knowing with just one look that their meeting
that day was "destiny."

During their courtship and the beginning of their
marriage, Julia found Max's subtly escalating control
over her to be flattering. He "loved her so much" that
he wanted her all to himself and was even jealous of
any time and attention she paid to her family and
friends. He "loved her so much" that he had strong
opinions about how she dressed, how much makeup
she should wear, and how she wore her hair. He
"loved her so much" that he insisted she not work so
that she could concentrate on making a home for
them, and he would call her constantly throughout
the day to find out where she was and what she was
doing. He "loved her so much" that he was terrified of
losing her to another man and hysterically accused
her of cheating on him with everyone from their gar-
dener to the manager of the grocery store where she
shopped.

She was hoping he'd feel more secure about her
absolute devotion to him when their twins were

born, but instead it only seemed to shorten his temper even more and make it harder for her to please him. She was "fat," he told her, and "letting herself go," and having babies was "no excuse." The house wasn't quite as meticulously kept and meals weren't quite as punctually prepared as they were before she had two infants to take care of, and again, that was "no excuse." After all, here he was working hard to provide her with a lifestyle anyone would envy, while she "didn't contribute a dime" to the household (she'd stopped pointing out that it was at his insistence that she hadn't pursued a career, because it only made him more furious), and how was he supposed to feel appreciated when she just "laid around all day not doing a damned thing"? He hadn't bargained on a "fat, lazy, sloppy" wife, so if he was spending more and more evenings away from home with "friends" rather than coming home to her, she had no one to thank but herself. And furthermore, he was tired of her being depressed all the time. What the hell did she have to be depressed about, for God's sake?

When he actually began hitting her, she only took it as more proof that she was a failure as a wife and a crushing disappointment to this man she was "destined" to be with, this man she knew she'd spent past lives with and devoted this life to. On the rare occasions when she'd sneak a call to her mother or sister or one of the few close friends she still had, needing to talk, all they did was tell her to leave him. As if she could, as if she wanted to, as if they were able to understand how much she loved him and how perfect her life would be someday if she just hung in there and loved him enough to inspire him to change back into that man who used to treat her so well and adore her so completely. Max was right: she was better off without these "outsiders," who only wanted to "interfere," break up a marriage, and put the innocent twins through the pain of a divorce.

The passing years only made things worse, not better, and the twins were starting to become hyperactive, anxious, aggressive, and often frightened by the many loud, sometimes physical fights their parents had. It was on their behalf that Julia came to me. Max would have never approved, and she'd made up an elaborate story to get out of the house long enough to make the appointment. But she was convinced that if I would regress her, and she could review the other lives she'd had with Max, she'd know how to help him and make him happy, and her own happiness and their children's happiness would naturally follow.

As you might know from a few of my past books, I've had my share of personal experience with an abusive marriage, and I have *very* strong opinions on that subject—not as a victim but as a survivor who finally walked out with nothing but my two young sons and the clothes on our backs. I knew exactly what her past-life history with Max really was, but I also knew she'd have to experience it for herself to believe it. And I wasn't about to shade her regression or influence it in any way. So I kept my mouth shut (not the easiest thing for me to do, let's face it) except to tell her very sincerely how glad I was that she came, turned on the tape recorder, started relaxing her, and simply said, "Let's go back and see if Max is really back there somewhere."

He was. Several times.

In their first life together, they were somewhere in the Middle East in the thirteenth century. Max was a judge of some kind who ordered Julia's eyes to be poked out when her husband wrongly accused her of looking too long at another man. In another life, Julia and Max were brothers in Spain. Max murdered a romantic rival but managed to get Julia tried and executed for it. In yet another life, Max was Julia's sexually abusive father, and she killed herself when she discovered she was carrying his child. And finally, Max was Julia's husband by an arranged marriage. He eventually took their only child and disappeared with another woman, and she never saw him or her son again.

"No wonder I recognized him the minute I saw him," she thought out loud an hour later. "So maybe in this lifetime I'm supposed to finally work things out with him."

"Or finally get so tired of being his victim that you refuse to put up with it anymore and walk away," I said.

She started to cry. "You don't understand, Sylvia. I love him."

"I do understand. I've been there. And for one thing, love isn't enough. For another thing, it's easy to confuse love with the feeling of an intense connection, and with your history together, even though it's literally cost you your life before, why wouldn't you feel intensely connected to him? But most of all, let's say it is love. Don't you think the lives of your children are too high a price to pay?

"He would never hurt them," she answered quickly.

"You're absolutely sure of that? Or is that just something you tell yourself to justify staying?" I couldn't resist adding a truth from my own life. "And for what it's worth, my sons have thanked me a thousand times for proving to them when they were little boys that nothing was more important to me than their safety."

Her eyes turned cold, and she stood and headed for the door with a dismissive, "I have to go."

I followed her to the door and stopped her just long enough to hand her a slip of paper. "Here," I told her, "hang on to this. Hide it somewhere, but keep it handy in case you want to use it. You'll find my hotline number on there. You can call twenty-four hours a day, and my ministers and I will help you. In the meantime, just promise me you'll keep praying that anything you've brought over from a past life that can hurt you be released and resolved in the white light of the Holy Spirit. If you won't do that for yourself, humor me and do it for your children."

She took the piece of paper and hurried out the door without another word. Maybe because looking at her was like looking in a mirror at myself in my twenties, I couldn't get her out of my mind. I thought about her, I worried about her, I prayed for her, and I had my ministers pray for her.

Eight months later I was in New England on a lecture tour when my cell phone rang. It was one of my ministers, telling me that a few hours earlier, Julia had finally called after Max left for work, and she and her twins were now safe at a women's shelter—Julia with her broken arm in a cast and one of her children with a badly swollen black eye.

That was five years ago. Julia and her children are thriving in another state. Max and his second wife, in the meantime, are awaiting trial for allegedly committing "reckless child endangerment and abuse." Their child is in foster care, and Julia prays every day for the welfare of that child, which could so easily have been one or both of hers, and for the strength to make sure that if her cell memory ever resonates again with the certainty of recognizing someone from a past life, she'll remember that sometimes that recognition means "Run!"

Mary Beth

• Always a Bridesmaid, Never a Bride

IF IT HAD HAPPENED ONCE, it had happened twenty times. Mary Beth would meet someone she was attracted to. Pretty, smart, and nice as she was, he would be attracted to her too, enough to ask her out. They would begin dating on a fairly regular basis, things would seem to be going well, and the next thing she knew, he would be telling her how much he valued her as a friend and asking her for advice about someone else he'd fallen in love with.

"Don't get me wrong," Mary Beth told me. "I'm proud of being a nice person and a good friend, and I'm glad men trust me enough to confide in me. But I'm thirty-two years old. I've had exactly one marriage proposal in my life, from a guy I barely knew who wanted to marry me so he could get his green card. The novelty of being the world's greatest buddy has worn

off. Just once I'd like to be the woman some guy is asking someone else for advice about. I know it's a long
shot, but I'm hoping you can help me figure out what
I'm doing wrong, or what there is about me that makes
it so easy for men to love me as a friend but so impossible for them to fall in love with me." She had read and
heard me speak about the power of cell memory, and
she had already come up with some possible past-life
scenarios that could be causing this problem. Maybe
she'd been a counselor at a boys' orphanage. Maybe
she'd been the mother to a lot of sons who turned to
her for advice. Maybe she'd been a priest, especially
gifted in hearing confessions, or a public defender
whom boys and men in trouble relied on to understand
and help without judging. But, as almost always happens, the real answer turned out to be the last scenario
Mary Beth would ever have anticipated.

It was the early 1800s, and Mary Beth, whose parents
were dead and who had no other family, was a teenage
girl, living and working in a house of prostitution. Contrary to the cliché of the poor, miserable, emotionally
tortured streetwalker, hiding her self-loathing and contempt for her clients behind a false smile and feigned
passion, Mary Beth enjoyed her life. She felt valued by
her clients. She felt appreciated. The sex act seemed like
a trivial, meaningless afterthought with these men, motions to go through before they confided their confu-

sion, frustrations, and heartaches, and Mary Beth kept their secrets as solemnly as she hid her familiarity with them when they happened to pass each other on the street. She and the other prostitutes in the house pooled their earnings, paid their bills right on time, took care of themselves and each other, and anonymously left a contribution before dawn every Sunday at the nearby church where they themselves were not welcome. Mary Beth died in that life of a venereal disease at the age of forty-four, with pride, dignity, and not a single regret.

She was incredulous immediately after her regression. "I was a *hooker?*" she kept saying. "And not just a hooker, but a *happy* hooker?" It almost seemed too ridiculous to believe, but Mary Beth couldn't ignore the absolute clarity with which she'd seen and felt that life, and the resonance deep in her soul that told her it was the truth. The longer she processed the information, though, the more sense it began to make and the more relevance it seemed to have to her current life. If her cell memory was sending her signals every time a new man came along that her greatest value to him would be as a compassionate confidante without the complications and burdens of romantic involvement, then of course she would be sending out those same signals for the men in her life to read.

"But what do I do about it?" she asked me. "How do I stop sending signals I don't even know I'm sending?"

I assured her that now that she'd made that connection, she wouldn't have to consciously do a thing. Now that her spirit mind and her cell memory could recognize they were still reacting to a life that was no longer relevant, they were guaranteed to make the adjustments themselves. All she had to do was keep praying to release any past-life lessons that weren't serving her well, go on with her life, and stay out of her own way.

It makes me smile that Mary Beth turned out to be a great example of the old adage, "Be careful what you want, because you just might get it." When I next heard from Mary Beth, eight months later, she was torn between two boyfriends, both of whom were very serious about her and both of whom had a lot to offer. She was calling to ask which one she should choose. She took my advice, gently dropped the tall blond landscaper with the strong jaw and deep-set blue eyes, and made a commitment to the shorter, huskier, darker, slightly less handsome film editor with two children and three dogs from a previous marriage. They've now added two children of their own and two more dogs to the household, and apparently he took it very well when she broke it to him that in reality he'd married a former British prostitute. "In fact," she told me, laughing, "we've made a pact not to hold each other responsible for anything from our pasts that happened before 1900."

Jay
Age Eight

- *Hyperactivity*
- *Breathing Problems*

I LOVE WORKING WITH CHILDREN, and they make wonderful regression subjects. Many of them—and I do mean *many* of them—still have conscious memories of their past lives and will happily tell you about them if you receptively ask a casual, "Who were you before this?" Fresh from The Other Side as they are, they haven't learned yet that there's anything inappropriate about discussing past lives, let alone that there are people who don't believe past lives even exist. As soon as they're able to communicate complete thoughts, they can tell us volumes about where they've been, what they've been through, who was with them, and what The Other Side is like. We're fools if we ignore them or dismiss their stories as silly nonsense. And before they're able to talk, we can help them enormously, especially when they're asleep and their ageless spirit minds are wide awake, by whispering to them to release any pain and negativity from past lives into the white light of the Holy Spirit.

When Jay's pediatrician referred him to me, he told me he couldn't find any physiological reasons for Jay's hyperactivity or for his breathing problems. Jay was an especially bright, sweet, good-natured child whose difficulties were causing him night terrors, panic attacks, and a lot of focus and discipline problems in school. The pediatrician had run out of tests, child psychologists, medication, and advice trying to help. He didn't use the words "last resort" about calling me, but we were good enough friends that it wouldn't have offended me if he had, as long as he got around to picking up the phone.

He was right, Jay was unbelievably likable, sweet and bright and inquisitive, with a great sense of humor. He was interested in everything in my office, especially some pictures of my grandchildren, which fascinated him. He wanted to know everything about them because, he informed me as if he were an old-timer talking to a contemporary, "I enjoy children, don't you?" Of far more significance, I asked him if he's happy. His answer was "I want to be." You can't ask for a more receptive subject than that, and it showed in the unquestioning ease with which he went "under." I told him I'd like him to go back and find the point of entry for his problems and smiled when he answered, simply and helpfully, "I will."

Immediately he began telling me about a life in South Carolina. He was a man, married to a "big woman named Anna, who's very nice." They had twelve children, and Jay remembered working hard taking care of horses on a ranch down the road from his house. He loved his children and enjoyed their noisy, active, playful company, especially when they all had supper together every night and went to church together every Sunday. But then one day Jay was called away to fight in "the war." He was sad to leave his family and their simple life and scared that he might never see his home again. He was assigned to a battleship and always carried a picture of his wife and children in the pocket of his shirt over his heart. He hadn't been gone very long when his ship was attacked, and Jay died instantly when a "piece of metal" hit his throat and crushed his windpipe.

The other life Jay remembered was in Denmark. He was a woman, married, the mother of ten children, living on a farm. Jay began quietly laughing as he talked about his family, and I asked him why. It seems he'd recognized his present-day mother as the most disobedient of his children in that life, and it amused him that now it was her turn to try to discipline him. When Jay was the female in Denmark, he was only thirty-four when he became bedridden with what turned out to be fatal pneumonia, and he recalled lying there alone, hearing the children boisterously going on with their lives outside the closed bedroom door and being too sick to be the mother they needed and deserved.

Jay listened very intently when I explained that after dying of a crushed trachea and of pneumonia, the cells of his body thought they were still in one of those other lives, and that's the only reason he had so much trouble breathing in this life. As for his hyperactivity, he was accustomed to huge, noisy families with lots and lots of children, and he'd been taken away from both of those families for reasons that weren't his fault. In this life, where he was an only child, the more noise and chaos he created, the more familiar his life would seem, and the more frustration he could release from those lives in which he hadn't felt at all ready to leave.

I called Jay's house a week later to ask how things were going. Both his parents got on the phone to tell me he'd had no breathing problems since our session, and they'd had a call from his teacher asking if we'd changed his medication, because he'd been much more focused and peaceful for the last several days.

Almost six months passed before I got another report on Jay, this one from the pediatrician friend who referred him. Not only had the breathing problems stopped completely, but Jay had gone through the whole winter without so much as the sniffles. He'd also successfully weaned Jay off his medication, and he seemed completely able and eager on his own to control his behavior. In fact, according to his mother, Jay's grades had gone from straight D's to B's and one C.

"I don't know what you did," he said.

I finished for him. "But it worked."

Snapshots

Not all clients need a long, full-blown regression in order to get to the heart of a problem that's rooted in cell memory. Sometimes just a snapshot from a past life is every bit as valuable in giving them all the information they need to heal.

Caroline, who suffered from an overwhelming **fear of insects**, uncovered a past death in which she was working in an African field in 1503 and was literally suffocated by a massive swarm of locusts.

Tom's **claustrophobia** vanished when he witnessed the cave-in of the coal mine in which he worked and died at the end of the eighteenth century.

Barry had a **fear of heights** until he remembered a fall from a coconut tree when he was a young boy in Hawaii in the 1600s. The fall broke his back, and, unable to move or get to help, he died alone beneath the towering fronds of that massive tree.

Anne-Marie was tired of being teased about her **phobia of food and drink that had been out of her sight**, even for a moment. She could no more eat in a restaurant out of sight of the kitchen, or return to a glass of water or wine after leaving the room where she'd left it, than she could sprout wings and fly. But once she revisited a previous death in which her meal had been poisoned by the very men who'd been hired to protect her from a small army of rebels who were plotting to assassinate her, the phobia quickly and permanently disappeared.

As I've said before, if a fear or an aversion is serious to a client, it's serious to me, with no exceptions.

When Ted came to me for help with his **fear of sharks**, he admitted that he felt a little sheepish about taking my time with it—after all, being afraid of sharks wasn't exactly unreasonable, and it wasn't as if sharks were hard to avoid in his life a good thousand miles from the nearest ocean. But he was tired of the nightmares and tired of making excuses to avoid friends' swimming pools as well as outings to a nearby lake, despite his rational mind scolding him for the nonsense of wondering if sharks were lurking there. And he was tired of the irony of being a clinical psychologist with such a senseless phobia.

All it took to cure him was a quick trip back to the year 1415, when Ted was a Spanish sailor. His ship caught fire and sank, and he was trying to swim to safety when a shark bit off his leg. He drowned before the shark came back to finish him off. The last few horrible moments of that life were all he remembered and all that needed to be released from his cell memory. Now, four years later, his nightmares are gone, he's had a swimming pool built in his own backyard, and, as his own private joke with himself, a large, professionally printed sign greets visitors to his pool that reads: "No running, pushing, excessive splashing, or sharks allowed."

It took Diana several minutes to even admit her secret problem, and even then I had to promise not to laugh. To her embarrassment, she was struggling with an extreme, lifelong **aversion to quilts**. Again, at first glance, that might seem as silly as sitting in the middle of Nebraska worrying about sharks. But even when she was an infant, Diana would begin trembling and crying at the sight of a quilt. As an adult she still broke out in a cold sweat and felt nauseous when she found herself anywhere near a quilt while shopping or in friends' homes. In her own words, she confided, "This is driving me crazy, and I'm really starting to get on my own nerves." Then she saw herself living in poverty in

Pennsylvania in 1780, a lonely, unhappy young boy working in the family business of making quilts. An older girl who worked there as well developed an obsessive crush on him and killed him when he rejected her. So much for her aversion to quilts. She still doesn't care much for them, but that's a far cry from the hysteria she'd spent her lifetime trying to overcome, let alone figure out.

Whether or not any of your own fears, phobias, or aversions are included in these documented stories, I hope you'll take heart in knowing that people just like you have literally put similar obstacles behind them forever, simply by releasing the cell memories that are causing those obstacles and finally giving the spirit mind the healing it yearns for.

And, thank God, the healing power of releasing negative cell memories doesn't end there. In fact, that's only the beginning. What it can do for physical health problems is every bit as remarkable and, in some cases, miraculous.

PART THREE

Health and Physical Challenges

Steve

• *Chronic Indigestion*

I SHOULD MAKE IT CLEAR right up front that Steve and I were already friends before I did his regression. He's one of my favorite people, and we joke about our good old days together, taking our Babylonian vaudeville act on the road. You might think our friendship made him a less-than-objective subject, but the truth is, there were two reasons I asked him to let me do a regression on him: one was that he's had a serious indigestion problem all his life I was hoping we could clear up, and the other was that I knew he'd never humor me by pretending to be "under" if nothing was really happening, or by claiming results after the fact if they weren't absolutely true. Stevie's neither a skeptic nor a pushover. He just assured me before we started that he had no expectations about being regressed, and he wouldn't be surprised or disappointed if it worked or if it didn't.

Almost immediately Steve was in a life in China. He was a farmer, raising crops and animals. His wife was no longer alive, and he lived with his two sons and his daughter, who were taking care of him because he was in his sixties and very ill with what we would now call stomach cancer.

I took Steve through his peaceful, welcome death, expecting him to start describing his next life. Instead, he found himself in the middle of the most beautiful green meadow he'd ever seen, and all around him, seeming to penetrate him to the core of his soul, was a brilliant white light that contained all peace, all wisdom, all purity, all love. He felt the touch of God in that light and understood for the first time what awe feels like.

That's all there was. Stevie's regression was over, and he sat up, ready to talk about it. He was his usual straightforward self. "Okay," he told me, "I have to admit, except for the meadow and the light, I never felt like I was really into it. I did what you asked and said the first thing that came into my mind when you asked me questions, but I have no idea if there was anything real about that whole China thing. Don't get me wrong, it was interesting. At best, though, it was like watching a movie that had nothing to do with me, and even at that, it wasn't all that clear. Sorry."

I assured him that no apologies were necessary. We tried. No harm, no foul. We never discussed it again, until Lindsay and I were well into this book, and I decided that since eight months had passed since Steve's regression, it might be especially interesting to have a follow-up conversation with him. To prevent his feeling awkward, or straining to think of something nice to say because he loves me, I asked Lindsay to do the update instead of me, since they go back even further than he and I do and there's no way he'd edit himself while telling her exactly what he thought and how he felt about the whole experience.

Bear in mind, Stevie's indigestion had been with him all his life, but the older he got the worse it was getting, and he'd accepted it as one of the unavoidable annoyances of turning fifty years old. The list of foods he could eat without discomfort later was growing smaller and smaller, but he was even more upset by the fact that if he ate after about seven-thirty p.m., he could count on a night of pain, cramps, and very little sleep. In a business and a social crowd in which dinner parties are almost a professional necessity and never start before eight o'clock, he was running out of excuses and finding himself excluded from more and more guest lists.

"I have to be completely honest about this, you do know that, don't you?" he said when he and Lindsay sat down together.

"We wouldn't have it any other way," she assured him.

"And the truth is," he went on, "when I'm careful with what I eat and what time I eat it, my indigestion is one hundred percent gone, for the first time in my life."

"What about when you're not careful?"

"When I'm not careful, and I pay no attention at all"—he paused and took a long, thoughtful breath before he finished—"it's at least seventy-five percent better."

"Starting when?" Lindsay asked.

"I still can't quite believe it, because I would have sworn I was almost just making up that whole story about China and stomach cancer as I went along, but there's been a huge improvement in my indigestion and my health in general since immediately after Sylvia regressed me. And I don't know if the regression had anything to do with this, but since then I've also started remembering my dreams every night, and that's never happened before."

If I'd been there, I would have told him how common it is for dreams to become more vivid after regressions. It's as if the spirit mind, having been fully acknowledged and given some exercise, refuses to go unnoticed anymore and almost shows off during sleep, when the conscious mind can't interfere.

Lindsay asked him if there had been any other changes he would attribute directly to exploring his deep, deep past. He didn't need time to think about it.

"The most amazing change, almost more than curing my indigestion, is that I've broken my habit of worrying. Things are far from perfect in my life. Work is sporadic, money's running low, if things don't turn around soon, I don't really know what I'm going to do. But I don't get anxious like I used to before that regression. I'm not being passive, I'm doing everything I can think of about my situation. But am I worried about it? No."

Lindsay was surprised, and impressed. Steve's never been a complainer, but she knew he was no stranger to worry and anxiety, no matter how quiet he tended to be about it. "Why is that? Was it the regression in general, or is there something you can point to that made you stop worrying?"

"Absolutely," he said. "It was that moment when I was in the meadow and felt that amazing, bright white light. There's not a doubt in my mind that I experienced that. It was as real as this chair, this table, this cup of coffee, and I can still retrieve that feeling instantly. Every time it even occurs to me to get anxious, or I find myself worrying about something, I just feel that light around me again and I know—I *know*—that everything's going to be all right. It's extraordinary. I'll never forget it, and I would never have imagined I was capable of this much peace of mind."

Stevie is a great example of how a regression can start with one goal in mind and end with other problems being resolved in the process. But he also illustrates why I never even try to lead any client through a regression. Psychic as I am, I can't begin to know as clearly as a client's spirit mind knows exactly what pain its cell memory is holding and where to go to heal it. It was Steve, not me, who insisted on finding the source of his stomach problems and then compounded his healing with a few moments on The Other Side to remind himself that whatever is making him anxious has already been taken care of at Home.

R.C.

• Chronic Chest Colds and Pneumonia

A T FIFTY-NINE, R.C. had given up on the idea of getting through a winter without two or three chest colds so severe that he'd be flat on his back in bed for weeks, rushed to the emergency room several times to help him get his breath, and being hospitalized at least every other year when the colds worsened into pneumonia. He took every precaution against illness he could think of, from massive doses of echinacea and vitamin C to flu shots to avoiding public places except his accounting office. It was bad enough celebrating four of the last six Christmases in intensive care while his wife, children, and young grandchildren spent their holidays making round-trips from home to the hospital. But his extended absences from work, combined with his age, were starting to make R.C. look much more expendable than the younger, healthier accountants in the company, and losing his job would place him and his wife in terrible financial jeopardy. To compound the household health and financial problems, his wife of thirty years, Camille, had been suffering since her early forties with terrible lower back and hip pain and sporadic numbness in her legs and feet and, despite medication, intensive physical therapy, and several surgeries, was in constant discomfort and unable to work.

"When Camille and I were engaged, I promised her that when I turned sixty, I'd retire, buy one of those huge Winnebagos, and spend the rest of our lives taking her anywhere she wanted to go. I'm turning sixty in three weeks, scared to death of getting fired from a job I can't afford to lose because I'm too sick to work about four months out of the year, and the only trips I can offer Camille are back and forth to the hospital. And now, on top of everything, no offense, but I'm sitting here with a psychic."

I smiled. "No offense taken."

He smiled back. "My doctor likes you, though, and I trust him, so I figured 'what the hell have I got to lose?' "

"Fair enough," I said. "Now, let's see if we can find out what's going on with you."

"I'm all ears," he assured me, nervous and tentative.

"I'm not going to tell you what's going on with you, R.C. You're going to tell me." I ignored the confusion on his face and started relaxing him toward hypnosis.

Twenty minutes later R.C. was describing a life in Africa. He was an architect, married, with three sons. He was happy, successful, and proud of being a good husband and father, and he wondered how he rated such a beautiful wife and such handsome children when he himself was short and slight and not very attractive. One day at the age of forty-six, he sent his family off on a holiday, where he would join them in a few days when he'd finished his work. He said good-bye to them and then headed off to one of his construction sites. He wasn't sure what happened or how, but he remembered sudden yelling and chaos and panic, and turning just in time to see a large stone from a pillar toppling down and hurtling toward him. It crashed into him and pinned him to the ground, crushing his chest, and he died wondering how and when someone would find his family to tell them what happened.

Next came a life in Wales, where R.C. was single and alone, putting in long, tireless days in the tiny coastal fishing village he founded. The work was hard, but it was also his passion, and he felt as responsible toward his fellow fishermen as if they were his own brothers. He and the other men in the village conquered the cold gray channel waters side by side, but they couldn't conquer the Vikings who attacked the unprotected little port one day from both land and sea, viciously killing everyone in their path, including R.C., who died instantly at the age of forty-eight from a spear that punctured his heart.

And then he was in Sweden, a proud soldier in the king's army. A fellow soldier wrongly accused him of theft and stabbed him repeatedly in the chest, hands, and legs one night while he slept. He survived his wounds but was no longer fit for military service. He lived the rest of his life in constant pain and poverty, a beggar in the cruel, frigid alleys of Stockholm, until he froze to death when he was fifty.

R.C. was one of those rare clients I call a somnambulist—in general terms, a sleepwalker, but in regression work, someone who has no memory of what he said or did while he was "under." He listened incredulously while I recapped the highlights for him and then slipped the tape of the session into his pocket to play later and prove I wasn't making this up.

"You never told me when this pattern of chest colds and pneumonia started," I said. "Do you remember how old you were?"

"The first time it became really serious, I was forty-eight," he answered. "Why?"

"Don't you see what your cell memory is doing?" I asked him. "In three past lives you suffered major trauma to your chest when you were right around that age. Your cell memory is just reacting to what it remembers, and creating severe pain in your chest because that's what it knows to do."

He thought that through and finally said, "Okay. I'm in no position to argue with you. But if I've had such a major breakthrough here, why do I feel the same as I did when I got here?"

"Just wait. Play the tape. And at the end of it, you'll hear me giving you a prayer to release any negative cell memories. Learn that prayer and make a habit of saying it a few times a day. Then call me after next winter has passed and tell me how many chest colds you had."

He was obviously intrigued but still not convinced, which was fine with me. I'd much rather have a client draw conclusions from their own experience than just blindly take my word for everything. I walked him out of my office and into the reception area, where a small, lovely woman with dark brown eyes stepped up to R.C. and anxiously asked, "How did it go?"

He answered with a noncommital shrug, then

turned back to me. "Sylvia, this is my wife, Camille. Camille, Sylvia Browne."

She smiled hello and extended her hand. Her subtle shyness was charming, but I could see the dull pain she lived with, which R.C. had told me about. Purely on impulse I said, "I'd love to help you."

It caught her completely off guard. "You would? Uh, yes, thank you, that would be great, but I know you have a long waiting list, so when—?"

"How about right now? Your husband was my last appointment of the day. I'd love to help you."

Camille

• Lower Back and Hip Pain
• Numbness in Her Legs and Feet

CAMILLE WAS FIFTY-SEVEN, two years younger than R.C., and still in love with him after thirty years of marriage. She'd been so worried about his health that she thought of her own decade of chronic pain and unsuccessful surgeries as nothing more than nuisances that prevented her from helping him as much as she wanted to.

"Your husband's going to be fine," I assured her. "Now, let's get you healthy so you can keep up with him." I knew she was very conscious of R.C. waiting for her in the reception area, so once she was "under," I told her to go directly to her points of entry.

She immediately went to a covered wagon train, making the difficult trip west from Virginia to California in 1851 with her husband, a farmer. She was twenty years old, with two young children, and excited about the adventure and the new lives the new land promised. They built their modest farm on sixty acres in northern California near the Nevada border. One day she and her children were walking across a field on their way to take food to a neighbor when they were ambushed by a small band of rogue Indians. Arrows pierced Camille's lower back and "left hip," and she laid there helpless, bleeding to death, beside the bodies of her children.

She next found herself in North Carolina, again on a farm, a happily married woman in her mid-twenties with no children. Every morning after her husband left for another hard day's work on their acreage, Camille would go riding on her beloved horse, a spirited chestnut mare named Athena. She remembered a gentle rain starting to fall one April morning, a reluctant decision to head home, crossing a shallow stream, and Athena bolting in panic at the sight of a water snake near the opposite shore. Camille was thrown, and found fairly quickly by a farmhand who'd become alarmed at the sight of Athena without her rider. Camille's hip and lower spine were shattered, and from that day forward she was paralyzed from the waist down, unable to walk or ride or care for her husband or herself ever again. She found it bitterly ironic that she outlived her husband. He died of an aneurysm when Camille was in her late forties, and she was tended to by the farmhands and their wives until she died, relieved to go, at the age of fifty-nine.

It was all laid out for her—the seemingly incurable hip and back problems she'd been suffering from, the sporadic numbness in the lower half of her body, her concern for her husband outweighing her concern for herself—all chronic and "untreatable" as her cell memories sent signals of pain, paralysis, and loss from other lives. Unlike R.C., she made the connections instantly and was excited about them when she left my office and reunited with him in the reception area. I smiled as I watched them drive away in the late-summer dusk, knowing they had some fascinating conversations and experiences ahead.

R.C. never experienced another chest cold, let alone another bout of pneumonia. Not one. He also never missed another day's work until he retired five years later. Camille, in the meantime, was soon strong and healthy enough to accept a job offer from a friend who owned a day-care center, where the children she loved kept her young, busy, stimulated, and active. Their last letter to me arrived a year ago. Its return address read "Anywhere, U.S.A.," and it contained a photo of them waving happily from the cab of their new motor home. The handwritten P.S. said simply, "What can I say—when you're right, you're right. Thanks! R.C."

Judith

• *Chronic Asthma*

JUDITH'S OCCASIONALLY SEVERE ASTHMA hadn't started until she was twenty years old, after the birth of her only child. She was now forty-three and had proudly just completed her medical degree, toward her dream of setting up a private pediatrics practice in her hometown near Cleveland. Her determination to conquer her asthma wasn't just for her own sake, it was also for the sake of any young future patients as well, whose illness, like hers, seemed unresponsive to medical solutions.

"If this works," she told me, "I hope you don't mind, but I want to learn your technique and use it myself when all else fails, to help asthmatic children I'll be treating."

Not only don't I mind, by the way, I'm thrilled when someone, especially a medical or psychiatric professional, is curious, creative, and flexible enough to care more about what works, without doing any potential harm, than they do about what science and traditional logic dictate. As I told Judith, I'm hardly what you'd call possessive with my information. What I know, you can know, and the more the merrier.

Her open-mindedness made her a wonderful subject, and she was "under" in no time, in Peru, a young boy, desperately poor, begging for food and coins on the steps of a stone church in the city. His mother, the only family he had, was absent for long periods of time with a variety of men who she hoped would take care of them but who always left her in the end. When he was thirteen, he contracted tuberculosis from the constant exposure, which went untreated and left him weak and frail. Finally his mother found work with a family in a town some distance away. They were crossing the mountains together on their way to the town when the air became too thin for him to breathe any longer. He died, grateful to be released from this empty, lonely life, and his mother buried him there on a high plateau.

She was a female in the second past life she revisited, in her teens in Germany. She lived alone with her very selfish, abusive, narcissistic mother, who demanded every moment of Judith's time and attention. There was plenty of money from an inheritance, which only made Judith feel more trapped—with no need to work, she also had no legitimate reason to escape the house and develop some semblance of a life of her own. As much as she disliked her mother and felt "smothered" (her word) by her, she also felt sorry for her and knew she'd never be able to live with the guilt of leaving this cruel woman to her self-imposed isolation. One night the two of them had a terrible argument, during which Judith threatened to leave. Her desperate, vindictive mother "snapped" and, while Judith slept, locked the door to Judith's bedroom and set their house on fire, in a homicidal-suicidal rage. By the time the fire was put out, Judith's mother had burned to death and Judith was dead of smoke inhalation.

I'm usually reluctant to generalize, but I've found that very often, clients with asthma and breathing problems are struggling with cell memories of difficult relationships with their mothers in past lives, either from neglect and absence or from excessive, "smothering" possessiveness. Judith was obviously no exception, and it was no coincidence that her asthma started shortly after her son was born and she herself became a mother. She admitted to me that the birth of her only child made her feel very conflicted. On the one hand, she loved the baby with all her heart.

On the other hand, she felt overwhelmed, scared and, to her shame, a little resentful about the staggering responsibility that motherhood presented her with. Judith's past-life history with the word "mother" was hard enough, but in her case, both mothers she recalled had also figuratively and literally caused her severe breathing problems.

Of course, only time would tell if the regression had had any lasting effect on Judith's asthma, but I suspected her results would be dramatic, mostly because of her openness, and that I would hear from her two or three months later at most. As it turned out, it was only a month later that she called to tell me that her asthma seemed to be gone and her breathing had been completely free, clear, and easy for the first time in twenty-three years. She wasn't quite confident enough yet to throw away her inhaler and her medication, but she'd ceremoniously moved them from the front of her medicine chest to a high shelf in a spare closet and hadn't given them another thought, let alone reached for them, in the last three weeks—two and a half weeks longer than she'd dared to hope for.

Believe me, I couldn't be happier for her. But I admit it, I'm even more excited about the news that Judith is studying to be a master hypnotist, along with her other postgraduate pediatric courses, and fully

intends to include past-life regressions in her arsenal
of weapons against any children's illnesses she comes
up against that don't respond to traditional treatment. "I'm living proof that it works," she said in a
recent letter. "What kind of doctor would I be if I
knew something worked but refused to offer it just
because it happens to sound weird?"

To the doctors who are reading this: it's a good
question.

Bo

• *Multiple Sclerosis*

IF YOU KNOW ME AT ALL, you know that Montel
Williams is my closest, most treasured friend, and
I love him in this life just as I've loved him in our
past lives together. In 2000, he announced to the
world that he was battling multiple sclerosis. So
when I say that nothing would please me more than
to find myself able to cure multiple sclerosis, I mean
every word, and I'm not overstating it. Until I can
make that claim, though, if ever, I'll always hold a
special place in my heart for those who suffer from
this cruel disease.

Bo was a handsome Texas rancher with a charming
drawl and a shy, lopsided grin. He was referred to me
by his doctor to see if I could help ease some of the
pain from the MS he'd been diagnosed with three
years earlier, and I jumped at the chance. Bo had

amassed a fortune thanks to pure hard work and wise investments, after a childhood of poverty and physical abuse. He was a combat veteran with a highly distinguished military record, he'd survived an attempt on his life by a greedy ex-wife and her gigolo boyfriend, he'd donated a kidney to his oldest son for a successful transplant effort, and he'd saved his ranch from natural disasters, market reverses, and an embezzling accountant. But never had he felt as threatened or as frightened as he had at that moment when his doctor spoke the words, "Bo, you've got multiple sclerosis." He was approaching MS exactly as he'd approached every other difficult challenge in his forty-six years, with a head-on, take-no-prisoners philosophy based on his premise that "God and I have a deal—I have faith in Him, and He has faith in me. If He puts an obstacle in my path and I don't put up a good fight, I'm not holding up my end of the bargain."

Bo was following his doctors' orders to the letter, had traveled extensively to explore treatment alternatives, was involved in several support groups with other MS sufferers, and was anonymously giving financial help to families hit hard by the disease. "Putting up a good fight" was an understatement, and the longer we talked the more I admired him. He'd also become one of Montel's biggest fans after learning that he and Montel were doing battle with the same insidious enemy. In the course of watching Montel's show, he'd seen me and decided that, while he wasn't sure how he felt about the psychic world, he was confident that we had our rock-solid love of God in common and that I wouldn't pull any punches with him.

"Want to become rich beyond your wildest dreams?" he asked me.

"Who doesn't?" I answered. "Why?"

"Cure me and I'll give you everything I own."

I put my hand on his shoulder. "Bo, I mean this with all my heart, if I could cure you, I'd do it for free. But a cure is coming within the next few years, I can promise you that."

He studied me, looking for some hint that maybe I was patronizing him, or offering some kind of glib false hope. Seeing instead that I meant every word of that promise, he smiled a little. Then, after a silence, he hesitantly cleared his throat and said, "You want to do a regression on me. Obviously that means you believe in past lives."

"Absolutely."

"Okay," he went on, "so let me ask you something. Let's say reincarnation and karma and all that other stuff are real. Does this disease mean I did something horrible in a past life, and now I'm getting paid back for it?"

"I could spend hours answering that question," I

told him. "But the short version is, *not a chance*. Before every life we live on earth, we write a chart for that life, which includes all the obstacles we're going to face in order to accomplish the goals we've set for ourselves."

He was incredulous. "Are you saying I chose to get MS?"

"That's exactly what I'm saying, and hard as this is to believe right now, the day will come when you'll even understand why you made that choice. In the meantime, though, remember this—only the bravest, most extraordinary spirits have the courage to set themselves up for serious challenges like yours. Do you really think some wimpy little wishy-washy spirit could handle what you're going through?"

"No. I don't," he finally said, with total conviction. "See? We haven't even started yet and I'm already feeling better. So how does this work? Should I tell you where I'm having the worst pain, or what?"

"Don't tell me anything, Bo. The less I know when we start, the more sure you'll be later that I didn't lead you or manipulate you or put words in your mouth. I'm not going to be giving answers to you, you're going to be giving answers to me. For now, all you have to do is make yourself comfortable."

I started with an especially long, deep, relaxing meditation, and saw the pain-tightened muscles in his jaw gradually uncoil, and he looked peaceful as I eased him into hypnosis. I prayed for his cells to remember that peace so that he could reclaim it whenever he wanted, then guided him into the past.

It was Tuscany, Italy. The year was 1041, and Bo was a fourteen-year-old boy with an identical twin brother named Garon who was blind. They were the oldest of twelve children born to solid, hardworking parents completely devoted to their family. On Sundays, Bo remembered, grandparents and aunts and uncles and cousins would travel from all over the countryside for great, noisy, laughter-filled feasts together, with more than enough love and affection and loyalty to go around. But as much as Bo loved all those happy, generous people around him, there was no one he loved more than his twin brother: that quiet, courageous mirror image of himself who never once complained about his blindness and always knew what Bo was thinking and feeling without ever having to be told. Bo had a gift for horticulture and spent long, happy days in the modest family fields and orchards, and he could almost feel the crops thriving in his care. Garon worked side by side with him, Bo's most eager student and helper, and the two of them shared secrets and stories and dreams until neither of them was sure where one twin ended and the other twin began. Every morning before dawn, Bo and

Garon would load a large wagon with their prized crops, the best to be found for miles and miles around, and take them to their father's stand at the open-air market in the town where he worked. Their father was proud of Bo's talent, proud of having the finest produce at the market, and proud of his twin sons' devotion to doing their part for the family's financial security.

Early one cold morning Bo and Garon had just arrived in town and were going back and forth across the narrow street unloading their wagon when another grocer's huge cart full of grain rolled off its wheel brace and began careening wildly down the street, unstoppable and headed straight for Garon. Confused by all the yelling and unable to see the cart coming, Garon stood frozen in the middle of the street, until Bo lunged to push his beloved brother out of the way in the nick of time. Garon was safe and unharmed. But it was too late for Bo. The cart rolled over him, its heavy wooden wheels crushing his chest and his legs. Bo's father and twin were at his side in an instant, holding him, crying frantically, and the last words Bo heard before he died were Garon's, asking him what happened and pleading with him to be okay.

Much later, after the regression, as Bo and I talked about the past life that had clearly touched him, he quietly asked, "Now can I tell you where the worst of my pain has been for the last six or eight months?"

I already knew, but I wanted to hear it from him, to be sure he made the connection. "Please do," I said.

"Across my stomach and upper abdomen, and in my legs, above the knees. Right where the wheels of that cart rolled over me. This past-life business may be new to me, but I saw that happen, clear as day, and it's no coincidence, that's for damned sure."

I explained cell memory to him, and we prayed together for his cells to release the awful pain they'd been holding on to for almost a thousand years. Then he lapsed into a long, preoccupied silence. Finally I asked what was on his mind.

"You want to know how real that experience was to me? I was just wondering whatever happened to poor Garon after I died," he confessed. "I hope he was all right."

"Tell me," I said, hiding a smile, "did he seem familiar to you, maybe remind you of anyone you know now?"

He thought about that. "Now that you mention it, even though they look nothing alike, there was something about him that felt exactly like my oldest son Wayne."

"Your oldest son in this life, right? The one you donated a kidney to?" Bo nodded, and I went on to tell him that he and Wayne had actually shared three past lives together. The first was the life in Italy. In the second they were best friends and business partners in Alaska, and in the third, in Morocco, they were inseparable female cousins. In every life they were devoted to each other, in every life Bo had been the caretaker of the two, and in all their lives together since Tuscany, Bo had been trying to make up for leaving Garon/Wayne so young and so suddenly, while Garon/Wayne had been trying to repay Bo for saving his life.

"You'd be amazed how much that explains about me and Wayne," he said with a grin. "In fact, he was with me when the doctor broke the news to me about my MS, and he took it harder than I did. He even said he wished it was him instead of me. I told him never to let me hear him talk like that again, but I suppose if you're right about this, he might be getting tired of outliving me." He looked at me. "I can just see the look on his face if I sat him down and said, 'Hey, Wayne, I went to a psychic today, and she says we're on our fourth life together.' He'd have me in an ambulance again in a heartbeat, but forget multiple sclerosis, this time I'd be off to a mental hospital."

We both laughed. "So don't tell him," I said. "But if you ever think I can help him deal with what you're both going through, just pick up the phone. If not, pick up the phone anyway. Keep me posted on how you're doing. And if you don't call me, I might as well warn you right now, I'll call you."

Bo and I have been in regular touch ever since. He continues to put up a brave, ferocious fight against his MS, continues to help other MS sufferers, and now includes them in his private daily prayers for God's help in releasing all of their negative cell memories into the white light of the Holy Spirit. His pain is no longer localized in his stomach, abdomen, and legs, and not a day passes when he isn't aware of the dramatic relief he feels in those very specific areas. Nor does a day pass when he fails to notice that he's no longer afraid, either of his disease or of dying, after that hour he spent back in Italy a millennium ago with a twin named Garon whom he now knows as his son Wayne.

As for Wayne, Bo brought him to a lecture I did in Texas last year. During the meditation Wayne thought he got a glimpse of an open-air market, lots of fruits, and vegetables on a wagon, and a brother who somehow reminded him of his father. As Bo put it so succinctly when he called to tell me, how about that?

Juliet

• *Anorexia*

J UST AS I WISH I could claim to be able to cure
multiple sclerosis, I also wish I had a foolproof
cure for anorexia up my sleeve. This complicated,
heartbreaking, and sometimes fatal affliction is as
hard to understand as it is to conquer, and its roots
can't always be found in any reliable hiding place,
including cell memory. Thank God, Juliet's case was
one of those that was willing and ready to expose
itself.

Juliet was twenty-one and had been anorexic for
almost four years, since her freshman year at an Ivy
League university. At five feet four inches tall, she
was frighteningly thin, weighing just over ninety
pounds. Her skin was gray-white, her long dark hair
looked as limp and deprived of nourishment as she
did, and there was no light at all behind her hollow

eyes. The psychiatrist who referred her to me described his three years of treating her as the most frustrating failure of his career. "I'm not giving up on her by sending her to you," he assured me. "I won't give up on her until she takes her last breath, hopefully when she's a very old woman with a houseful of great-grandchildren. But you've known me for twenty years. You know how I hate to lose. I'm afraid I might lose this one if I don't play my ace in the hole, and after your track record with some of my other clients, that's you. I hope you don't mind being called my ace in the hole."

"After everything else I've been called in my life? You must be kidding. Get her here as soon as you can, and I'll put her at the top of my 'urgent' list."

Adding to Juliet's physical problems was a severe case of chronic dysentery. She'd had "about a thousand" upper and lower gastrointestinal tests, all of which came back normal. "I'm so 'normal,' " she said, starting to cry, "I've had to quit school. I'm so 'normal' I barely have the strength to get out of bed in the morning. I'm so 'normal' my family bursts into tears every time they look at me. If I get any more 'normal' I'm going to die."

It wasn't self-pity, it was a statement of fact, and I knew death was starting to sound like the only relief available to her. Maybe if I could help her to discover why a beautiful, bright, talented, privileged young woman, with a brilliant future in her choice of professions and a loving, supportive family, would rather die of starvation than go on living, she could at least walk out of my office remembering what hope feels like.

As ill as Juliet's body was, her spirit mind was healthy, crackling with life and yearning to be heard. Even her voice changed once the regression was under-way, from the trapped monotone of the present to something vibrant, strong, and sure.

In the first life she returned to, she was a young Indian brave in the Pacific Northwest. She knew the thick forests for miles around as intimately as if she'd created them herself. She could and did survive alone in those forests for weeks at a time, away from her tribe in search of valuable pelts. Every tree and plant was a rich source of food and healing oils. Every broken branch and disturbed pile of leaves told stories as easy for her to read as a child's primer. The sky was her familiar guide and timekeeper, each breeze carried scents that defined every nuance of all that surrounded her, and even the silence of dark nights was full of secrets the land seemed to whisper for no one but her to hear. Her instincts were as finely tuned as those of the creatures she felt honored to live among, and she sensed the Divine Spirit in the earth, the sky, and the animals that all united to give her a home she considered sacred.

At every new moon she returned to her tribe's small village with skins and food. She held her family and the tribal elders in almost reverent respect, and she was privileged to be such a prolific contributor to their well-being. But after a few short hours at the traditional village feast of gratitude to the Divine Spirit for her safe return and for the generosity of His creation, she invariably became overwhelmed and claustrophobic in the company of all these people and their well-meaning but noisy expectations and stole quietly away again into the blessed thick forest, where she knew she belonged.

She was still young, in her early twenties, she thought, and on her way back to her village with supplies when a raging fever overtook her. She was almost unconscious when she was found and taken to her mother and grandmother, who tended to her with the help of a shaman, bringing her thick broth and homemade elixirs, none of which she could keep down. The whole village gathered around her, offering chants and prayers for healing, as she grew weaker and weaker.

"They're too loud," she told me. "Too busy and too loud. I can't hear."

"What can't you hear, Juliet?" I asked.

"The earth," she said.

She lingered for six endless days before "I was released and my spirit was received into God's peace." She was grateful, almost elated to go, and she was aware that many times in those six days her spirit had taken astral trips to the depths of her beloved forest to say good-bye.

Juliet revisited two other lives, in much less detail, during her regression. In one, she spent thirty years in solitary confinement for alleged treason and died of severe peritonitis, an abdominal infection, two unhappy months after her release from prison. In the other, she was kidnapped from a rural school playground in the early 1900s, sold into prostitution in Miami at the age of twelve, and was beaten to death by her captors when she was fifteen after she tried to run away.

In life after life, including her current one, Juliet was struggling with the issue of her *life theme*. Before each of our lifetimes, we write a detailed chart of the lives on earth we're about to embark on, kind of a road map for achieving the goals we set out to accomplish while we're here. We also choose a theme, from a list of forty-four life themes, that will define our essence, our primary driving force for that lifetime. All forty-four life themes and their descriptions are listed in my books *The Other Side and Back* and *Life*

on The Other Side, but for now we'll just focus on
Juliet's chosen theme: loner. People with a loner
theme can be perfectly social, visible, and publicly active, but their real comfort level is found in being
alone, where they're free to make their own choices
and, for the most part, control their environment.
Loners are at their loneliest when they're surrounded
by other people, particularly when those other people are strangers or mere acquaintances who can't offer any form of intimacy. Where others find comfort,
emotional nourishment, and stimulation in groups,
loners find irritation, confusion, and a draining inva-
sion of the small, private space they need to have
ready access to. The bottom line is a requirement, as
real for the loner as oxygen, for a readily available
option to control what's around them, even if it's just
for short periods of time. Privacy for them is about
recharging their batteries, replenishing their energy
supply, and being nourished by the sheer luxury
of making their own basic choices without input,
compromise, or interruption until they're ready to
handle them again.

In life after life, Juliet had gone from an environment of peaceful simplicity and some semblance of
privacy to an environment full of other people that,
for her, amounted to nonstop noisy, invasive, confusing overload. Adding to the messages her cell memory

retained from those lifetimes, private simplicity was safe, but being surrounded by other people meant death.

And now, in this life, Juliet had gone from her parents' house, where her family didn't especially relate to her need for privacy but respected it and accommodated it as best they could, to a major, prestigious, bustling university that was fully prepared to provide for every student's intellect and ambition but wasn't equipped to provide for every student's specific emotional individuality. As far as Juliet's cell memory was concerned, these dorm rooms and roommates and crowded classrooms and communal meals and seemingly required sorority rush parties and activities were no different from the Indian village, the confounding "freedom" of society after thirty years of the solitary confinement she frankly preferred, and the abusive total control of her kidnappers. She felt threatened, she felt surrounded, exactly as she'd felt in those other lives. Her body, taking its cue from the cells that fed it information, was doing what past experience knew to be inevitable and simply preparing to die. After three previous deaths that involved attacks on her stomach and abdomen, what could be more natural than that in her case, the path to dying was through dysentery and starvation? With a loner theme and the reality that privacy is essential to emotional nourishment, why wouldn't relentless deprivation of that privacy put itself on obvious display in the form of physical malnourishment? And if at the core of the loner theme is a need to control the immediate environment, wasn't it almost predictable that Juliet would seek out the one thing—how much or how little she ate—that no one else but her could dictate? Ironically, everyone's concern over her anorexia only made it worse. If she thought she'd been inundated with people before, it was nothing compared to the crowd that seemed constantly gathered around her, trying to make sure she ate, trying to make sure she made it to doctors' appointments, trying to analyze her, trying to get her to open up about what was really causing this awful problem, trying to give her well-intentioned advice, and on and on and on, all out of love and all making her more determined than ever to escape.

I need to stress this again: I'm not suggesting that at the core of every case of anorexia lies an unrealized loner theme, or even that every case of anorexia can be cured by past-life regressions. But in Juliet's case, thank God, it worked. The first step was to acknowledge and release all the negative information her cell memories were infusing her with. The next step was to cooperate with her loner theme in a positive way, instead of fighting it and even scolding herself for it.

As soon as she got back to school, she moved out of the dorm into a tiny studio apartment off campus that would have felt claustrophobic to most people but felt like paradise to her—there simply wasn't room there for anyone else. She politely declined sorority invitations with a nonjudgmental "it's not for me, thanks." She sorted through her few extracurricular activities and eliminated those that were characterized by crowds and noise and social functions, and instead she focused on such relatively secluded activities as a mentor program working with an inner-city child, answering a battered woman's hotline, and even the ultimate private sport of golf. She spoke with her favorite professor and volunteered for a lab research project he'd offered, which she loved and excelled at. Not by magic but by assuring her cells in meditation that she intended to live, not to die, she eased her way into eating again, was managing three meals a day within a month, and three months later had gained almost ten pounds, while her dysentery completely vanished.

It's been six years since my regression with Juliet. She's still slender but thirty-five pounds heavier than when I met her, and is a happy, healthy, enormously successful forensic pathologist, a brilliant blend of her academic gifts and her ability to thrive and excel when given long hours of uninterrupted concentration.

As for the psychiatrist who sent her to me, I'll always honor my promise to keep his identity confidential, especially after his call to congratulate me on Juliet's dramatic recovery, which ended with his rather sheepish request for a regression for himself. That regression cleared up a bad case of chronic psoriasis on his left foot and ankle, which we discovered had been burned to the bone in a house fire in Bulgaria in 1507. The burn became infected, and the infection killed him.

I've now made a commitment to teach regression hypnosis techniques to both that psychiatrist and his dermatologist, who'd spent two years treating that psoriasis and declared it incurable. As they told me in a recent cowritten letter, "We figure that if this cell-memory treatment catches on, it could either put us out of business or quadruple our clientele. We prefer the latter."

Rich

- *Severe Neck Pain*
- *Motion Sickness*

Rich is yet another example of how, far from guiding clients during a hypnosis session, I'm really just along for whatever ride they take me on. I help my clients to the doorway to their past, I give their regressions some form of structure, I keep them safe from emotional harm while they're "under," and I help them process the experience and release the pain they've come across when the regression is over. Other than that, it's their journey they take, not mine, and I'm often as surprised as they are at where it leads.

Rich was thirty-two, a fairly successful drummer who did freelance work for recording studios and a variety of bands. Contrary to the cliché image of a freewheeling, long-haired, pot-smoking, itinerant band musician, Rich was a clean-cut, funny, articulate, drug-free, nicely dressed family man with a mortgage, a Volvo, a wife and two children he adored, and a third child on the way for whom he was personally building a nursery. His often excruciating neck pain had started without warning when he was twenty-five, while he was umpiring a neighborhood softball game for a group of friends and their children. There was no obvious cause, no trauma, no collision with a base runner, not even an odd twist or turn to his body he was aware of. As he described it, "it just hit out of no-where, like I'd been whacked in the back of the neck with a hammer." He'd been x-rayed, MRI'd, treated by chiropractors, sports medicine therapists and acupuncturists, shot with cortisone, and prescribed everything from anti-inflammatories to muscle relax-ants to heat packs to cold packs to ultrasound, and as far as he was concerned, he was actually worse off seven years later than he was when the pain first hit— now, instead of just an aching neck, he had an aching neck and higher medical insurance rates from all his doctor visits.

"I swear I would just live with this if I had a choice, but it's interfering more and more with my work. Try playing drums when you can't move your head. Take it from me, I've been doing it off and on for years, and it's—" He paused, laughed a little, and continued. "Well, pardon the expression, but it's a real pain in the neck. Anyway, I don't have any more time to waste running back and forth to doctors who can't seem to help me. I need help, I need it now, and I need it fast."

"Great," I said, chuckling. "No pressure there. Although frankly, that's exactly the approach I believe in anyway, and I'll do my damnedest. Just out of curiosity, though, besides wanting to stop hurting as soon as possible, what's the rush?"

"It's kind of a good-news/bad-news joke," he said. "The good news is, I just signed a contract for two months' work with a ballroom dance band on a cruise ship. The bad news is, I just signed a contract for two months' work with a ballroom dance band on a cruise ship. Two months of steady paychecks is a godsend anytime in my line of work, and it almost feels like a miracle with a baby on the way. But I don't think there's a chance in hell I can handle two straight weeks of this pain, playing four-hour sets every night, let alone two months. And on top of that, just to give you the real punch line to this story—I have almost terminal seasickness."

"Lie down," I insisted, with only half-kidding urgency. "We've got work to do."

The year was 1716, and Rich was a crewmate on a pirate ship off the coast of the West Indies. His employer was very cruel, not only to his victims but also to his crew, who were systematically beaten, starved, and tortured for even the slightest infraction, real or imagined. Most of the men onboard were outlaws themselves and willing to tolerate almost anything for their share of the take and for the amoral lawlessness of piracy. But Rich and a handful of others decided that even death was preferable to life under these conditions, so one moonless night they slipped quietly over the side of the ship and into the cold rough ocean, their goal being to swim to shore and escape. They had no way of knowing there was a traitor among their rebel group who had alerted their employer of the plan. They were quickly apprehended by the employer's loyalists, easily reaching them in small boats. The lucky ones were killed immediately in the middle of the ocean. Rich and two or three others were captured and brought back to the ship, where they were bound, gagged, blindfolded, and thrown into the hold. Rich didn't remember how many days or weeks they were tortured and starved, but he did remember lying on wooden planks in the dark, in horrible pain from the beatings, cramped and weak from hunger, unable to brace himself as the ship pitched wildly in a fierce storm. He was grateful when finally, while he was barely conscious, he was carried up from the hold and thrown overboard to drown.

I never make personal comments during a regression, but I remember being impressed that Rich had signed on for this cruise job at all, with a cell memory of ships as hideous as that. I also knew that once he released that experience, he'd never feel a twinge of seasickness again.

Next Rich was in a friendly, happy, familiar pub, sitting at the bar, surrounded by good friends. He was aware of a window, through which he could see Buckingham Palace in the distance. He was twenty-five years old, unmarried, and made a comfortable living as a farrier. (I had to look that up after he left. A farrier, it turns out, is a blacksmith.) He was vaguely aware of two men entering the pub, one of whom hated Rich for getting him fired from his job for stealing. Rich was enjoying himself and chose to ignore the man's glares in his direction. Suddenly he felt a crushing blow to the back of his neck and collapsed to the floor. He opened his eyes just long enough to see the man standing over him with a thick iron tool that looked like a crowbar. He died two days later from acute swelling of the brain.

I jotted that down: "died from neck injury at twenty-five in past life, severe neck pain started at twenty-five in this life." It didn't take a psychic to make that connection. Moving on, I told Rich to describe what he saw after his death in that life. There was a long silence, and then he began telling me about a stone bench near a crystal-clear waterfall in a vast, impossibly beautiful garden. He could see a white marble building with pillars far away, at what seemed to be the entrance to the garden. Rich had never read my book *Life on The Other Side*, so he had no way of knowing that he was giving me a perfect description of The Other Side's Gardens of the Hall of Justice.

"What are you doing at the stone bench, Rich? What's going on around you?" I asked.

"I'm sitting. Waiting. I was asked to come here," he told me. "And now there's a man coming toward me. I've been waiting for him. He's young, about my age, but his hair is white, down to his shoulders, and he has on a long goldish-yellow caftan or robe or something like that."

"Do you know who he is?"

"He says he's my Spirit Guide. His name is Aaron."

I sat forward in my chair. Aaron, I knew, was the name of Rich's Spirit Guide in this life, not in the past as I was expecting. I asked him if he happened to have a time frame for this visit to the Gardens.

"Now," he said. "It's happening right now."

I was fascinated. It seemed Rich had gone from a regression right into a present-tense astral trip, with his spirit taking the opportunity to leave his body for a jaunt to The Other Side. I fought the temptation to interrupt by pointing that out to him and instead just asked, "Why did he ask you to come there, Rich? Do you know? Is he saying anything?"

He silently listened for a minute or two without saying a word. When he spoke again, he sounded intrigued and almost amused. "He says I wasn't just reminded of that experience in the pub to get rid of my neck problem. It was also a warning to be more alert and pay more attention to what's going on behind me so that something like that doesn't happen again."

When Rich came up from his relaxed state and we'd had a good talk with his cells about letting go of those painful memories so that he could enjoy his upcoming cruise ship job, I told him how unusual it is for a Spirit Guide to come through like that during a regression and give him a handy tip for future reference.

"Remember, your Spirit Guide can read the chart you wrote for this lifetime," I pointed out. "I've ignored my Spirit Guide, Francine, in the past, out of pure orneriness, and I've always ended up regretting it."

He was confused. "Okay, let's say I did write another injury from behind into my chart. If I wrote it, how do I know I shouldn't just go ahead and let it happen, for some reason I'll come to understand later?"

"Or," I answered him with a question, "how do you know you didn't chart this session with me so you could be warned about it and prevent it?"

He nodded, and before he left I made him promise to keep in touch, about the cruise and most definitely about the birth of the baby, which I promised was going to be a chubby, healthy boy.

Almost four months later a long handwritten letter arrived. The cruise had gone beautifully, without a hint of seasickness. As for Rich's neck pain, it vanished within a few days of his regression and had never returned. And there was one "little event" from the cruise that he couldn't wait to tell me about. He and the band were on the large riser in the ship's main ballroom. They were in the middle of a set, and their bandleader/pianist was introducing the next song, when Rich heard a muffled combination of creaks and pops above and behind him. He looked toward the noise and then dived out of the way a split second before the twenty-foot velvet drape behind him and its heavy iron rod came crashing down, destroying Rich's drum stool before it hit, and cracking the teak platform floor. "I was fine, other than a case of the shakes for about the next week," he wrote. "But if I had any doubts before about my

Spirit Guide, they're sure gone now. If you and he didn't save my life, you definitely saved me a broken neck."

There was a picture enclosed of their chubby, healthy week-old baby. They named him Israel.

Nora

- *Asthma*
- *Chronic Back Pain*

Nora was thirty-five and two months pregnant. An earlier pregnancy had ended in a miscarriage, and she was determined to carry this one to term, including getting and staying as strong and healthy as possible for the duration. She needed help with the asthma she'd suffered with since her early teenage years, and she was also hoping we could get to the bottom of the back pain that had plagued her since a very minor fall on a small hill during a ski lesson. She was left terrified of skiing and loathed everything about the sport. She knew the back pain was likely to get worse as her pregnancy progressed, but according to the specialist she'd been seeing, there was absolutely nothing wrong with her. She became so frustrated at her last appointment when he told her she was "just imagining" her pain that she couldn't resist announcing, "I'm sorry, my mistake for bringing you a back problem that's too tough for you to handle. Oh, well, I'm seeing a psychic next week who I'm sure can take care of it for me." He snapped back that if she wanted to throw her money away on "some crackpot psychic," he wouldn't dream of stopping her.

Believe me, she got her money's worth and much, much more in our ninety minutes together.

She found the key to her asthma almost immediately, in England in the year 1110. She was fourteen years old, crouched in the corner of a very small, cold, dark room underground, and every labored breath she took was heavy with the musty odor of wet earth and mold. She was in hiding, sure that she would be either imprisoned or executed if she were found, for what was then considered to be "a crime against the Church." It seems she was part of a small, covert group who worshiped the Mother Goddess, called themselves Essenes, and studied the "witch-craft" we now commonly call herbology and aroma-therapy. They had been "raided" one night during a worship service, and Nora had escaped and locked herself for days in this cramped root cellar that kept her safe from "the establishment" but filled her lungs with spores of fungus and mildew that caused her countless debilitating illnesses until she died four years later of acute pleurisy.

Nora's point of entry for her back pain happened in France in 1822. Nora was eight years old, small for her age, as petite and ethereally beautiful as her mother, who was a celebrated chanteuse. Nora's brother Gerard was five years old when Nora was born. He was spoiled, arrogant, and physically took after their tall, handsome, muscular father, who owned many of the nightclubs at which their mother sang. Before Nora was born, Gerard was invariably taken by his parents to these clubs at night, where he'd be fussed over and waited on like royalty while his mother sang in her glittering gowns and his father moved among the tables greeting the fawning patrons like a powerful, charismatic puppeteer animating his amusing collection of marionettes. But when Nora arrived, it was easier and less demanding for two such social parents to hire a full-time nanny and leave both children at home every night. Suddenly Gerard's cherished outings with his parents stopped, and he had to share their attention and affection during their few hours at home. As far as Gerard was concerned, his life had gone from feast to famine, and it was all because of this uninvited infant intruder. He despised her from the beginning. His behavior toward her vacillated between icy disregard and what little pain he could inflict without getting caught and punished.

Nora was healthy enough and independent enough to decide at a very early age that her brother wasn't a very nice person, his resentment toward her was his problem, not hers, and she wasn't about to let him stop her from having the happy life she had every intention of living. Nora and Gerard coexisted in their undeclared cold war until Nora's eighth birthday. A fabulous birthday party was waiting for her in the backyard, with ponies and clowns and music and presents and her many friends. She had just started toward the long curved staircase of their house toward her party when all of Gerard's contempt and jealousy boiled over, and he ran up from behind her as fast as he could and pushed her. She rolled and careened in a violent fall down the hardwood stairs until she landed at the bottom, her back broken, in unbearable pain. She saw Gerard turn away at the top of the stairs and disappear, and she was dead before the doctors arrived.

It wasn't hard to figure out that there's not much difference between the action of falling down a long staircase and skiing down an icy hill when skiing is a new, scary concept. Her cell memory clearly thought there was no difference at all, and cued her body that the result of that action is that her back hurts her terribly, no matter how minor the skiing fall itself really was. Nora told me later that she's fought a life-long fear of heights, she's never ridden on an escalator without her palms getting sweaty, and she drove her husband crazy when they were shopping for a house several years earlier because she refused to even look at anything that wasn't all on one level.

I was taking Nora past her death at Gerard's hands when she suddenly murmured, "I need to meet my child."

"The child you lost?" I asked her.

"The child I'm carrying. Is that possible?"

I explained that we could ask for any spirit she wanted to talk to, but there was no guarantee that that particular spirit would show up. Nora's Spirit Guide was a man named Dominick. I told her to choose a specific place for the meeting to happen, picture it in as much detail as possible, and then ask Dominick to invite the spirit of Nora's unborn child to meet her there. The rest would be up to the child.

Nora described a footbridge over a crystal brook in the middle of an endless, breathtaking meadow. Beyond the meadow she could see a massive white marble building with what seemed like a mile-high expanse of steps leading to its entrance. I asked her if she knew where she was.

"It looks familiar," she answered, "but I can't place it."

I wasn't about to interrupt to tell her, but she was at the entrance to The Other Side, where she'd been many times before. The distant white marble building she saw was the stunning Hall of Wisdom, which is every new arrival's first stop.

She was alone at first. Then a dark-haired woman appeared beside her. The woman had a flawless olive complexion, huge brown eyes, an angelically round face, and a graceful hourglass figure.

"Who is she?" I asked.

There was a confused frown on Nora's face. "She says her name is Rachel, and she's the daughter I'm pregnant with."

"Do you believe her?"

"I'd like to. She's beautiful. And she does have my husband's coloring, and my mother's eyes. I guess I just wasn't expecting to meet a grown woman."

I smiled and explained that everyone on The Other Side is thirty years old. But she didn't have to take my word for it, or even Rachel's. In seven months, when her baby was born, she'd know whether this experience really happened or not. "Whoever she is, she was nice enough to come and meet you," I pointed out. "So you might as well see if she has anything else to say."

"She wants me to know that she's the same baby I was carrying before, it was just the wrong time for all of us, but everything will be perfect this time. And this will be our fourth life together. We've been best friends twice, we've been brothers, and the last time around I was her son." She paused, then added, "She says she can't wait to get here, that she's due in November, which is true, but she'll be born three weeks early."

By her own admission, Nora's meeting with her unborn daughter couldn't have seemed more clear and more real, and her skepticism was purely a case of being afraid to believe it. She might just have made the whole thing up out of her desperate hope that she'd make it through this pregnancy successfully. I assured her that I didn't blame her or anyone for skepticism, since I'm a skeptic myself. But she could take it from Rachel, and from me as a psychic, that she'd welcome a healthy baby girl into this world in October. Time would tell whether or not that prediction was accurate.

We didn't have to wait that long for the first results of her regression. Within a month, Nora reported that both her asthma and her back pain were completely gone, to the point where she was already wondering whether or not she'd "just imagined" suffering from them in the first place.

Of far more significance, I received a birth announcement seven months later, celebrating the arrival of a perfect six-pound, twelve-ounce girl named Rachel on October 24. She had olive skin just like her father, and big brown eyes that reminded everyone of her maternal grandmother.

I'm sure that someday Nora will tell her daughter about a pre-birth meeting on a footbridge over a crystal brook in the shadow of a white marble building. And if she does it while her daughter's still a child, there's every chance in the world that Rachel just might remember it.

There's no question that undiagnosed illnesses and pains are the number-one concern of all my regression clients and the doctors who refer them. But it's worth repeating—cell memory is *not* the cause of each and every health problem that comes along, and no psychic, including me, should ever be used as a substitute for a responsible health-care professional. As I often point out, God made doctors too, and I'll always insist on working with them, not instead of them. So please be diligent about your physical and mental well-being and, when something goes wrong, remember that I cherish every client who walks through my door. Given a choice, however, I do not want to be the only call they make.

PART FOUR

*Positive Cell
Memories
and Cell Memories
from This Life*

IN CASE YOU'VE BEEN WONDERING, there's a very good reason to specify that our cells should release into the white light of the Holy Spirit any *negative* memories they've brought over from a past life. Our spirit minds are gifted with perfect retention. They have total recall of everything they've ever experienced. As we've seen, that certainly includes physical and emotional pain, both resolved and unresolved. But it also includes times of happiness, triumph, health, and peace, from lives here on earth and on The Other Side, and those positive cell memories can be enormously valuable to the lives we're living now.

And speaking of the lives we're living now, please don't get the impression that all the cell memories we react to every minute of every day come from lives before this one. We've seen time and time again that our realities aren't limited to what our conscious minds remember, that our realities are a constant blend of conscious memories and each moment our spirit minds recall and infuse into our cells. Our conscious minds are flawed, forgetful, and very self-protective. As best they can, they believe what they want to believe, interpret facts to their own advantage, and are unreliable when it comes to what they've experienced. If what's happened to us were limited to our conscious memories, then apparently none of us spent time in the womb, none of us went through being born, and all of us started our current lives about the age of three.

So, negative and positive, from some past life or from this one, our spirit minds hold it all for safe-keeping, and our cells take their cue.

Jill

• *A Career Crossroads*

J ILL WAS THIRTY-FOUR and very successful, on paper. She was hired at twenty-one, fresh out of college, by a major Midwest marketing firm, and had risen in the ranks over the years to achieve a coveted executive position. A six-year marriage in her twenties had ended amicably and without children, and she used her share of the sale of their house to buy a small, attractive town house. She had a fairly active social life, but her career kept her traveling and busy enough that she wasn't interested in finding, let alone making room for, another "Mr. Right."

There was just one problem—she wasn't happy. "I feel like an ingrate," she told me, "because I know how lucky I am, I know I have no business complaining. But I feel like I've just been going through the motions for years now. My job stimulates my head, but nothing about it touches my heart, and I'm realizing more and more that life is too short to let myself go on like this with no place to put my passion. I'd change careers in a heartbeat if I could figure out what I'd be good at and feel passionate about at the same time."

"Law enforcement," I said.

"I'm serious," she replied.

"So am I," I insisted. "You have a great mind for puzzles, clues, unraveling mysteries, that kind of thing. And I doubt if anyone has ever successfully lied to you. You're like a natural walking polygraph machine. You'd make a terrific detective, and, take it from me, I work with enough law enforcement agencies to promise you'd be needed and appreciated."

She was more amused than convinced. "I don't know, Sylvia, it seems like an awfully big leap from being an avid true-crime reader to becoming a cop."

"Law enforcement doesn't necessarily mean 'cop,' Jill," I pointed out. "You asked me what you could be good at and feel passionate about at the same time, and I'm telling you. You're unhappy because your marketing career doesn't give you an outlet for your life theme, which happens to be 'justice.' "

"Justice, huh?" She wasn't arguing. "I can see that, actually. Nothing makes me crazier than people getting away with things that are just obviously unfair. I've always wondered where that came from."

I asked if she'd like to find out, and she smiled, openly intrigued.

Twenty minutes later she was in a city in New England. It was the spring of 1923, and she was a forty-one-year-old man named Morgan—she wasn't sure if that was the first name or the last, she just knew it's what everyone called her in that life. Morgan was a doctor, a general practitioner with a small private practice, tireless, fiercely loyal to his patients, and known for traveling any distance for a needed house call. Morgan was married to a shrewish, miserably unhappy woman named Hesper, who complained bitterly about being the wife of "the only doctor in the East who isn't rich." She hated the endless hours his practice demanded and seemed to hate it even more when he was at home. She expressed her raging resentment by spending money far beyond their means, having numerous affairs, and helping herself to the virtual pharmacy he kept in their home for his emergency calls, often sharing the drugs with the other men in her life.

When Hesper was found beaten to death in their home, with fresh needle marks in her arm, Morgan was arrested and charged with first-degree murder. Everyone knew he had a motive, there was no sign of forced entry into the house, the drugs and syringe involved certainly originated from his supply, and because he'd spent the night in question traveling from one distant patient to another, he had no alibi to speak of. He was innocent, and beyond outrage at the suggestion that after devoting his life to saving lives he could be capable of taking one. Even his own lawyer believed he was guilty and withdrew from the case when Morgan refused to accept a plea bargain. In the course of conducting his own meticulous investigation with the help of his friends while preparing to represent himself, Morgan uncovered several clues and facts the police had overlooked and managed to free himself by proving the identity of the real killer: a married lover of Hesper's whom she'd threatened to expose when he tried to end their affair.

Jill was amused when we talked after her regression. "I have to admit," she said, chuckling, "that sounds like something I would do under those circumstances."

"Can you consider the possibility that it's actually something you *did*?" I asked her. She shrugged a little, not dismissing the idea but still skeptical. "Which would certainly explain where your 'justice' theme came from. And thanks to cell memory, it could indicate a real talent for solving mysteries that carried over from that life to this one. It's up to you whether you do anything with that talent or not. But you came to me to ask about a career change, and now you have my word for it, and your own word for it, that some form of law enforcement is at least worth considering."

It was more than four years before I heard from Jill again. I thought about her from time to time and wondered what happened, and while I didn't have a doubt in my mind about the validity of my reading and her regression, I wasn't a bit sure that she hadn't gone off and dismissed the whole experience as an hour of nonsense. So it was an especially pleasant surprise when a thank-you note arrived from her out of nowhere, with a business card enclosed bearing her name and the simple legend "Private Investigator" beneath it. According to her note, she's making less money than she did as a marketing executive, but she's never been happier or felt more worthwhile, and she's just added a very prestigious law firm to her quickly growing client list. I couldn't agree more with the conclusion of the note: "I wake up every morning looking forward to the day ahead. Now, *that's* success."

Seth

• His Child's Illness

Seth was the thirty-year-old father of a beautiful four-year-old daughter named Ashley Rose. He'd been a mechanic in his father's auto repair shop since the day after he graduated from high school, which was the same day he married his high school sweetheart and Ashley Rose's mother, Janice. Seth and Janice, a hairdresser, worked hard, lived simply, and yearned for a child. Ashley Rose was born on their eighth wedding anniversary, and no two people ever felt more blessed or loved their baby more than they did. There was no warning and no genetic reason to have seen it coming when, at the age of three, Ashley Rose became desperately ill with what was discovered to be a rare kidney disease. She was a strong child and fought her illness like a tiger, but it finally became apparent that a transplant was the only thing that could save her.

"I need to know if they're going to find a donor and if my little girl is going to be all right," he told me. "And please don't give me false hope. What I don't need right now is the Hallmark card version of how this is going to turn out. That's why you're the person I came to. I've seen you in action on TV. You don't back down from bad news. You'll tell me the truth, and the truth is what I need."

"They'll find a donor, Seth. In about four months. Amazingly, from the same hospital your daughter's in now. The first compatibility tests they run will be in-conclusive. Make them do the tests again. They'll come back positive the second time, and the trans-plant will be a success. Your daughter's going to be fine."

He studied me, then asked, "You mean that, don't you?"

"Yes. I mean that," I said. "In fact, it's a promise. She'll come through this with flying colors. Frankly, I'm more worried about you than I am about her."

"Oh, no, don't tell me something's wrong with me," he groaned.

"Not physically. Physically you're fine. Emotion-ally, this is a lot tougher on you than you're letting anyone see."

"It's tough on me, it's tough on my wife, it's tough on all of us," he shot back, more defensively than he meant to. "How could it not be?"

"I don't want to talk about all of you, I want to talk about you." I kept my voice flat and calm. He wasn't going to open up about this very easily, and I didn't want him any more upset than he already was. "Why don't you tell me what happened yesterday?"

He was shocked. "How do you know about yesterday?"

"I'm psychic." I smiled. He smiled back a little before I went on. "You ran out of the hospital. Do you want to tell me what that was about, or do you want me to tell you?"

He tried shrugging it off with a dismissive, "I hate hospitals."

"Everyone hates hospitals," I pointed out. "Not everyone has a panic attack when they're in one."

He looked away and ran his hand through his hair, his exhaustion showing. "I don't understand it. It makes no sense. I can't even count the number of hours I've spent in various hospitals with Ashley in the last year, and I was scared for her. It's been a nightmare, but I did okay. But then yesterday, Janice was in Ashley Rose's room with her, and I was walking up the hall to get coffee when I overheard these two nurses talking. One of them said, 'I don't think she's going to make it,' and the other one said, 'Neither do I.' Just like that. That's all it took. I don't even know if they were talking about my daughter. But all of a sudden I just froze. I couldn't walk another step. I broke out into a cold sweat, I got dizzy, I started shaking, my ears started ringing, my legs felt like rubber, and I was sure I was going to faint. You'd think a hospital would be the most convenient place to faint, but my wife already had enough to deal with. I couldn't scare her like that, so I turned and ran out of there as fast as I could and just sat in my car for two hours until I felt strong enough to go back to Ashley's room and at least pretend to be relatively normal again."

I asked if he told his wife what happened.

He shook his head. "I haven't told anybody. I'm too ashamed of myself."

"Why? It's not as if you planned a panic attack. You were obviously blindsided by it."

"Blindsided or not, my daughter's very sick, my wife's every bit as exhausted as I am. Anything could have happened in those two hours, and where was I? Hiding in my car trembling and hyperventilating like a damned coward. I've never thought of myself as weak before. It's a terrible feeling."

"You're not weak, Seth," I assured him. "And panic

attacks don't usually happen in a vacuum. Something triggered it, I promise you."

"Can you tell me what it was?"

"It'll have more of an impact on you if you tell me. Would you like to try?"

He was more than willing, open to anything that might help. As I began the hypnosis procedure and saw how easily he was going "under," I thought for the thousandth time that the human mind is a marvelous thing. So often the more preoccupied and in pain it is, the more receptive it is to finding a way to make sense of its pain and begin healing. I also thought, for the ten thousandth time, how vulnerable the mind is and how obscene it is for therapists and hypnotherapists to suggest or steer a vulnerable mind that is searching for help and useful information toward conclusions that have nothing to do with the truth. We've all seen, heard, and read about people "remembering" everything under hypnosis from childhood molestation to a parent committing a murder. Some of those memories are real, but just as often they're the result of a hypnotherapist wanting to make a name for themselves at the client's expense. The difference can usually be found in the questions and comments of the hypnotherapist, not of the client. That's why I *always* give my clients a tape of their session, so that they and anyone else can listen to it after the fact and be absolutely sure I'm just a facilitator and not a source of any memories that reveal themselves.

Seth and I started slowly back through his current life, beyond his conscious memories and into his infancy, moving toward his birth as the gateway to his previous life, when he stopped at the age of eighteen months. He remembered being very sick and very weak, with frequent seizures that were taking their toll on his tiny heart, and lying in the hospital nursery surrounded by machines and strangers with white masks over their mouths. His mother and father were there a lot of the time, but one day when they were gone he remembered two nurses beside his crib. The nurse who was changing his diaper said, "Poor little guy, I hope he'll be okay," and the nurse who was looking at his chart said, "From what I hear, there's not much chance of that." He remembered the helpless terror he felt when he heard that, lying there unable to move or speak, wounded that someone would say something so casually careless right in front of him, as if he'd already ceased to exist. But as the days went by, his terror turned to anger, he became determined to survive and, with the help of a change of medication, he was taken home healthy and thriving a week later.

Seth was shocked by the clarity of the memory

when we talked about it after the regression. He knew from his parents that he'd been hospitalized for seizures when he was an infant, but he had no idea what caused them, and he certainly had no conscious memory of the experience.

"You had a severe lactose allergy," I told him. "Ask your parents. They'll confirm that. Thank God someone was diligent enough to figure it out. But look at the parallel between what that nurse said beside your crib in the hospital and that conversation you heard yesterday in the hall. You're already afraid and vulnerable because of your daughter. There you are in a hospital again, and all it took was that trigger to send you back to the life-threatening panic you felt but couldn't express twenty-eight and a half years ago."

"Or maybe I projected that panic onto Ashley Rose and my terror of losing her," he added.

"There's another point about that experience I hope you'll pay attention to, Seth."

He asked what it was.

"When you were only a baby, you beat the odds and fought your way back from an allergy that a lot of infants don't survive, even when it sounds like some people around you were ready to give up on you. That doesn't sound like the weak, pitiful coward you claimed to be when you first got here."

It made him smile, even chuckle a little when he

observed, "That's true." As he left my office a few minutes later, he made three promises to me: to let me know why he was hospitalized at eighteen months of age, to warn the hospital staff not to utter a single negative word within earshot of Ashley Rose, and to keep me posted about her condition and their search for a kidney donor.

Promise number one was kept with the news that Seth's hospitalization had been for seizures caused by an allergy to lactose.

Promise number two prompted him to tell Ashley's doctors and nurses about his reading and his regression. Curious, a few of them began giving constant positive reinforcement and encouragement to Ashley Rose and the other seriously ill children in the pediatrics wing, even when the children were sleeping, and noticed improvements they described as "extraordinary."

And then there was promise number three. I was in St. Louis, in the middle of a lecture tour, when my office called with a message from Seth marked "urgent." I could hear the excitement in his voice the instant he answered the phone.

"Guess what—you were wrong," he announced, too obviously happy about it for me to panic.

"That happens," I said. "Any psychic who tells you

it doesn't is a liar. So what was I wrong about, ex-actly?"

"You said they'd find a kidney donor for Ashley Rose in four months. It only took three." The surgery was a complete success, he told me, and his daughter had been officially declared "out of the woods."

Sometimes it really bothers me when I'm wrong. This was not one of those times.

Carrie

• *Her Pregnancy*

EVERY READING and every regression fascinates me. Each one is different, each one is its own true-life story, each one matters, each one has limitless potential for discovery, each one expands my knowledge as I hope it expands the knowledge of the client, and each one offers as few or as many results as the client wants. And then, every once in a while, I get back the same glimpse of spiritual magic I try to give, and am blessed with another reminder that there's no age limit on feeling awe.

Carrie was in her late twenties, with a mane of long, straight natural blonde hair that I knew she'd been envied for all of her life. She was happily married, seven months pregnant, and glowing with the life inside her.

"Before we get started," she said as she sat down, "I have to ask you—do I look at all familiar to you?"

It's one of my least favorite questions. I'm not that great with names and faces to begin with, and my life doesn't lend itself to getting any better at it. "I'm sorry, but no, you don't," I told her. "Why?"

"The first time I ever saw you on television, I burst into tears, and it's kept right on happening ever since."

"I know I trigger a lot of different reactions in people," I said, "but bursting into tears is a new one. Was it something I said?"

She shook her head. "It started before you said a word. It was like running into an old friend, like this big wave of comfort hitting you out of nowhere, even though I was sure there was no way we'd ever met. Maybe I recognized you from a past life or something. But I called your office that first day I saw you, and I've been waiting for this reading for almost two years."

For the record, I hate the length of my waiting list and wish I knew what to do about it.

At any rate, we quickly shrugged off her instant recognition of me as one of life's little mysteries and proceeded with her reading. This was her first pregnancy, and even though she'd been almost fanatically diligent about her health and prenatal care, she was anxious to be assured that the delivery would be normal and her baby would be fine.

"How about nine pounds, two ounces?" I smiled. "Will that be fine enough for you?" She grinned and gave a mock agonized groan. "You already know what it is, don't you?"

She nodded. "Do you?"

"It's a girl," I said.

"It better be," she told me, "or I've been wasting a lot of time needlepointing the name 'Rebecca' on everything I find myself sitting next to. We're naming her after my mother."

"Was she tall, blonde, very slender, long legs, a runway model's body, wore her hair in a ponytail, perfect posture, a fabulous laugh?" I asked.

"Why?"

"Because she's standing right beside you. And she's very excited about this pregnancy."

"I can confirm everything you just said about her except the laugh," she said. "She died when I was four. I've got a million pictures of her, but I don't remember her laugh." She paused and then added, "I suppose it's too much to hope that—"

"That she's coming back in the form of the daughter you're carrying? No, Carrie, it's not her. But she'll be around, you can count on it. Watch your baby when she starts staring at something you can't see, or starts giggling for no apparent reason, or talks to what looks to you like thin air. Your baby will see her grandmother as clearly as she'll see you."

"I'd give anything if I remembered my mother," Carrie said, as much to herself as to me. "She was apparently an incredible woman, and my family has told me all sorts of great stories, but I'd love to have just one memory of my own to share with my daughter about the grandmother she's named after."

I couldn't think of a lovelier reason for a regression, and Carrie was thrilled at this chance to experience her mother firsthand. Several minutes later she was in her childhood home in Ohio, in her yellow bedroom, lying in bed, surrounded by stuffed animals. It was the night of her fourth birthday party, and Carrie was holding her favorite gift, a blue life-size poodle wearing a beret. Her mother was sitting beside her in bottle-green satin pajamas, long hair down, and Carrie could feel it lightly brushing against her cheek as her mother leaned down to pull the covers more tightly around her.

"Is she saying anything?" I asked.

"She's singing," she told me, then listened, smiled, and added, "Badly. She has this soft, wispy voice, and she can't carry a tune. But she doesn't care, and neither do I."

"Can you hear what she's singing?"

"Not very well, but it sounds a little like—" She

trailed off, listened again, and chuckled. "I think it's a Beatles song."

"She has good taste."

" 'Octopus's Garden.' " We both laughed at that. Thousands of Beatles songs to choose from, and her mother came up with "Octopus's Garden" as a lullaby. I was kind of sorry I'd missed her myself.

Suddenly Carrie took a quick, short breath and announced, "Wait, I just remembered something else. I used to have this recurring dream when I was a child. I think it was after my mother got sick. But it didn't seem like a dream, it felt more like I was flying around visiting people during the night."

I knew that's exactly what she was doing and asked, "If I said the words 'astral travel' to you, would they make sense?"

"That sounds right," she said. "I remember having my spirit taking little running steps and then jumping to get itself going, kind of like Superman did when he took off to fly. I don't remember ever looking down to see my body lying in bed, but I do remember I loved flying above the ground and seeing the treetops beneath me. And I had a favorite person I loved to visit. She would wait for me by this waterfall in the middle of a beautiful garden. She was tall and strong, with wise, compassionate eyes and large breasts. No matter how sad I was feeling, she could always make me laugh, and she would always say, 'You're safe with me,' and I felt safe there. She must have been an imaginary friend or something, and I guess I saw her a lot, because I'd go running to Mom the minute I woke up the next morning and tell her, 'I went flying with Bun again last night.' "

I wasn't sure I'd heard her correctly. "You saw who?"

"Bun," she repeated. "I'm not sure where that name came from; I just knew to call her that."

It was one of those rare moments when I found myself speechless. Bun isn't exactly a common name, and, I informed her, it happens to be my nickname on The Other Side. I might have written it off as a coincidence if I believed in coincidences and if she hadn't had such an immediate reaction of comforting familiarity the first time she saw me. I choose to believe that throughout my life my spirit has used my sleeping hours to travel to a waterfall on The Other Side to meet the spirits of children and other future clients and, even if it's just for a few moments in a dark night, make them feel safe.

Carrie's daughter Rebecca was born two months later, weighing in at nine pounds, four ounces. Wrong again—I missed by an ounce. And I really hope the baby likes "Octopus's Garden," because I have a feeling she's going to be hearing it as a lullaby every night for many, many years to come.

Jane

• *Marital Problems*

I LEARN SOMETHING from almost every reading and every client, and my hour with Jane was definitely no exception. We've all met people with whom, from the moment we meet, we share a mutual dislike and just plain annoy each other without even trying; especially if life has made it impossible for us to avoid each other. Every time I think of those people in my life, I remember Jane.

Jane and her husband, Ryan, had only been married for four years and were already separated. They were both nice, hardworking people, and they loved each other. The seemingly insurmountable problem that had caused them to separate was such a cliché that Jane even smiled apologetically as she said it: Jane's mother-in-law, Saundra, had become so intrusive and unbearable that Jane had moved out, and

Jane was hoping I could assure her that somehow Saundra was going to either get a life of her own or, better yet, vanish into thin air.

"I know it sounds ridiculous that I could let anyone get to me so much that I'd walk out on my marriage," she admitted. "But I can't take one more minute of this. Ryan's an only child. He and his mother have always been close. She became a widow while Ryan and I were dating, and we both felt sorry for her and started inviting her out to dinner with us once or twice a week. Next thing you know the three of us were practically inseparable. I thought it would be nice to ask her to help me plan our wedding. Who knew she would end up taking the whole thing over? She chose the church, the minister, the colors, the bridesmaids' dresses, the music, the menu, the orchestra for the reception. She even went behind my back after I'd ordered black stretch limos for the wedding party and changed it to white ones because she finds black limos depressing."

I interrupted, already knowing where this was going. "And let me guess—if you complained, Ryan accused you of being ungrateful when his mother was going to all this trouble." She nodded. "Please tell me she didn't go with you on your honeymoon."

"Oh, no," she said, "that would have been too easy. Instead, she decided to suddenly have unexplainable chest pains and check herself into the hospital three days into our honeymoon, and we immediately flew home."

"Heartburn?" I asked, already knowing the answer.

"Heartburn," she confirmed.

That was only the beginning. Concerned about his mother's health and not wanting her to be lonely, Ryan found Saundra an apartment two blocks from his and Jane's new home and gave her a key to their house, which was all the permission Saundra needed to make their house hers. She was a constant presence, letting herself in whenever she wanted, never bothering to knock, let alone call first, and she completely took over, all in the name of "helping." She rearranged everything from the furniture to the kitchen cupboards to Jane's dresser drawers. She "surprised" them by having their house unnecessarily recarpeted in a color Jane hated while Ryan and Jane were on a two-day business trip. She even hired a housekeeper on the premise that Jane "just didn't have a knack for cleaning" and then criticized Jane in private to Ryan for not doing enough around the house. Through it all she was infallibly sweet to Jane, but only when Ryan was in the room. Behind her son's back, Saundra was often snide, cruel, and condescending to Jane, and quick to quote anything Jane said in retaliation to Ryan, usually through injured, innocent tears, which invariably led to an argument between Ryan and Jane.

"He keeps saying, 'She's done everything for us, she loves you so much, and all she gets back from you is resentment. Whatever your problem is, get over it.' I finally decided that the only way I could get over it is to leave. But I really do love my husband, and I really believe if it were just the two of us, we'd have a wonderful marriage. I'm just hoping you can tell me if we're ever going to get that chance, or if I should give up and move on."

"Needless to say, she doesn't love you, she knows exactly what she's doing, and the day you moved out was the day she won, as far as she's concerned," I assured her. "But it's not the usual possessive mother-in-law who doesn't want to let go of her son. This is very personal between you and her. You and Saundra have a fascinating history together."

"Like what? I killed her in a past life, and she's using this life to get back at me? Or better yet, she did something horrible to me in a past life, and I get to pay her back by killing her in this one?"

She was kidding, but the thought of it wasn't completely unappealing, and we laughed a little before I answered her. "If I tell you," I said, "you'll never believe me. Why don't we take you back and let you see for yourself?"

She willingly agreed, and before long she was moving back through her life, from adulthood, through her awkward teen years as an army brat, through her happy childhood, and into the womb she was so reluctant to leave that doctors finally had to induce labor to force her out five days past her due date. I then told her to go to the point of entry where this war of nerves between her and Saundra was first declared. There was a long silence, followed by a confused frown.

"I see us," she announced. "Saundra and me."

I asked what they were doing.

"We're laughing. We like each other. In fact, we're good friends." Even under hypnosis, she sounded a little incredulous about it. "We're working together. Tending animals. They're not in cages or anything, they're free, in this green valley, with mountains all around. The air is fresh, and the sky is the color of sunset. I can't even put into words how beautiful it is."

"Do you know what year it is?" I asked her.

She thought about it, then, "Year? There's no year. There's no time. There's just—now."

That could only describe one place. "Where are you, Jane?"

"I'm Home," she said. "On The Other Side." There was awe in her voice.

"So on The Other Side, you and Saundra are friends."

She nodded. "We're talking. Making plans."

"About what? Can you hear the conversation?"

"We've decided we want to spend another lifetime on earth. We've both got something we feel we need to work on, and we understand each other so well that we're going to chart our lives in such a way that we can work on it together so we'll be sure we don't make it too easy on each other, or just walk away before we've learned what we need to learn."

"And what is it you two are here to learn?"

She began to laugh. It was infectious, and momentarily I was laughing too, without knowing why.

Finally she got out the word that was the life theme and lesson she and Saundra had agreed to help each other with before they came here this time around: "Tolerance."

We were laughing again after her regression. "Tolerance," she repeated. "In other words, I actually asked Saundra to be in my life and see if she could drive me crazy so I could learn to deal with it. Well, she's been doing a great job of it, I'll give her that." After a pause she added, "Poor Ryan."

"Why 'poor Ryan'?" I asked.

"He's kind of the unwitting victim in all this, isn't

he? He's just this terrific man we used to bring us into each other's lives."

"And now you know why he's so terrific," I pointed out. "If he were a jerk, you probably would have walked away years ago, and Saundra probably wouldn't find him so impossible to let go of."

By the end of our time together, Jane had decided to go back to her husband and make their lives together work. "For starters," she told me, "how many times in my life am I going to be given the chance to be married to a great guy?"

"I'm not disagreeing with you, Jane, but I should warn you—Saundra's not going anywhere. In fact, she's going to be alive and well for another thirty-two years. Are you sure you're up to dealing with her?"

"As my mother-in-law? No. But as an old friend I made a pact with? I'll find a way."

Jane did go back to Ryan. Saundra is still impossible. And every time Jane thinks she can't take it anymore and is ready to explode, she remembers being on The Other Side with her friend, carefully planning all this, and laughs, and gives Saundra a hug.

"That works on two levels," I told her when she called with this report several months after we met. "Spiritually, it's a lovely thing to do. From a purely human standpoint, it must drive her crazy."

She tried to muffle it, but I still heard her chuckle.

"Sylvia, you heard the agreement at the same time I did. I'm not just here to learn tolerance from her, I'm here to teach it, too. What kind of friend would I be if I didn't give her something to tolerate?"

Like I said, I still think of Jane and smile.

Matthew
Age Four

• *Chronic Depression*

A<small>ND THEN THERE WAS</small> M<small>ATTHEW</small>, who was a perfect example of positive cell memory and present-life cell memory both coming out in the same regression. Matthew was four years old and one of the most gorgeous children I've ever seen. He'd been blind since birth, and while his parents were willing to move heaven and earth to help him, providing him with therapists and doctors and a specialized preschool, he didn't seem to be adjusting well. He wasn't angry, just sad and introverted and unusually quiet for an otherwise healthy little boy. One of his preschool teachers knew my work and recommended me to Matthew's mother, Grace, who ached for her child to be happy and was wide-open to suggestions.

It didn't take Matthew long to get comfortable

with me. The instant I said hello to him, he lit up and said, "I hear you on TV. You're funny." I get that from children all the time, especially my grandsons Willy and Jeffrey. "Psychic-shmychic, big deal, just keep those laughs coming, okay?" That's not a complaint, believe me. Not only could I not imagine living this life without a sense of humor, but nothing puts children at ease more quickly, and that included Matthew. In fact, when Grace suggested he might open up more if she stayed in the room with us, Matthew spoke up before I could and politely excused her with a simple, "We'll be fine, Mama."

When we were alone, I did find Matthew to be quiet, but he was also sweet and smart and eager to please. I explained a little about hypnosis and what we were going to do, and that I wanted him to tell me all about himself so that we could be friends. Just like my granddaughter Angelia at that age, he couldn't say his r's yet either, and he reminded me so much of her when he answered, "All wight."

Like most children, he was a wonderful, wide-open subject, guileless and fearless, and within just a few minutes his breathing was deep and steady, and he was completely content.

"Who were you before this?" I asked. It's a question young children are remarkably responsive to, with or without hypnosis, because their past lives are still so recent and so much more familiar than the lives they're living now.

"A tall man with dark hair," he told me. "I make music."

"What a wonderful thing to do. How do you make music, Matthew?"

"A lot of people sit in front of me with horns and drums and things, and I tell them when to play and when to stop."

"You were a conductor?"

"Yes. A conductor. Like this." He began waving his arms in the air. This four-year-old boy who'd been blind since birth knew exactly what a conductor at work looked like.

"You must know a lot about music to be a conductor," I said.

"I do. I'm very good," he informed me with the charm of a child's candor. "I can write (again, like Angelia, pronouncing it "wyte") it, and I can play it on the piano. I love music."

"Do you still love music now that you're Matthew?" I asked.

"I think so. I can't play anymore, though."

"Sure you can," I told him. "You've just forgotten how, that's all. A teacher could help you remember."

"No, I mean I can't."

"Why not?"

"Because I'm blind." The sadness in his voice was heartbreaking.

"Who told you being blind means you can't play music, Matthew?"

"Mama. She says I can't do a lot of things other children can do."

I moved to sit beside him and put my arms around him. He nestled into me. "You know what?"

"What?" he asked.

"Your mama was wrong," I insisted.

"Did she lie?"

"No, Matthew, she didn't lie, she was just mistaken. Every once in a while, we don't mean to, but we moms say something that's wrong. I remember I was wrong once, when I was just about your age." He giggled. "I'll tell you what—how about if I talk to her?"

"Maybe you could make her feel better," he said.

"Is she sick?"

"She's sad. My daddy's sad, too. All the time."

"Why?"

"Because of me."

Yes, I was definitely going to have a talk with his mother. I held him for several minutes, stroking his hair, and told him that sometimes our spirits remember things that help us and sometimes they remember things that hurt us, and he was only going to remember things that help him, like the music he loved, from now on. God would take the things that hurt him and surround them with His light of love so they would disappear and never hurt him again.

Finally I put him into the capable hands of my staff, who were practically standing in line to meet him and entertain him while I spent some time alone with Grace in my office. I explained that Matthew believed he was a useless little boy trapped by all sorts of limitations other children don't have and that she and her husband were sad all the time because of him. "I'd be quiet and depressed too if that's what I thought my world looked like," I said.

She was crying. "Sylvia, we adore our son. We would lay down our lives for him in a heartbeat."

"I know that," I assured her.

"I admit, we're pretty much stretched to the limit, financially and emotionally. But he's worth it, believe me. Hard as it is, we've devoted ourselves completely to Matthew's blindness."

I've seen clients go through this a thousand times. It's an easy trap to fall into. "Maybe that's the problem," I suggested. "Maybe if you'd devote yourselves completely to your bright, beautiful, sensitive child, it might be easier on all of you. You might even start having fun with him, and I think you'd see a big turnaround in him if he felt he were living with two people who just plain enjoy his company." She was listening, taking that in, and as long as I had her attention I decided I had nothing to lose by pressing on. "Now, Grace, what's this about telling him he can't do things other children can do? Why would you want to put limits on him like that?"

"I honestly have no idea where he got that, Sylvia," she insisted. "I've gone out of my way never to say anything like that to him or around him. I can't even imagine hinting at it. Matthew's doctor and I even talked about that when he broke the news to me that the blindness seems to be irreversible. My first reaction was grief and anger at how unfair it was that this innocent baby didn't get to live a completely normal life. But our doctor gave me a lecture about the importance of positive reinforcement, and I haven't said or allowed a negative word about it since."

"Where was Matthew when you had that meeting?" I asked.

"He was with me," she said. "But, Sylvia, he was only seven months old."

"In *this* life he was only seven months old. But there's a spirit in there that's as old and wise as the rest of us. It's amazing how much they understand and remember."

She was quiet for several moments. Finally, open

but not completely convinced, she tentatively asked, "So what do I do about it?"

"Just apologize and tell him you've realized how wrong you were. He'll understand that, too. And then, if I were you—is there any way you could arrange to get him a piano?"

"A piano? Why?"

"Because I think he'd enjoy it. Call it a hunch for now, and if it turns out I'm right, I'll tell you all about it."

"There's no way we can afford to buy one," she told me. "Although my sister has one she might be willing to loan us for a while."

"Perfect. Ask her," I said. "Then turn him loose with it for a few months and call and let me know what happens."

Eight months later I got a thank-you note from Grace with a photo of a beaming Matthew and his parents, posed beside Matthew's piano. There was a tape enclosed of a song he'd written, that all the children in his preschool class had learned and sang at their last-day-of-school party. It was a very simple song, hardly destined to become a hit or a classic, and the lyrics didn't begin to rhyme. But it was about a very happy little boy with very happy parents who are proud of him, and it may be the sweetest song I've ever heard.

* * *

You've read story after story after story of other people's experiences with the impact of cell memory on their physical and emotional health, good and bad, from this life and past lives, and the freedom they found in releasing those cell memories that are doing them harm. But I would never consider this book complete unless I acted on my conviction that what I know, you can know. In other words, there's no cell-memory story as interesting or important as yours, and all you have to do now is uncover what your story really is.

PART FIVE

The Secrets of Your Own Past Lives

THE JOURNEY

We all know that knowledge is power. So it's only logical that self-knowledge is self-power. The more we know about ourselves, the more effective people we'll be and the more comfortable we'll be in our own skin. Understanding what motivates us, what repels us, what we yearn for, what we need to avoid, and *why* we think and feel the way we do can make all the difference in the world in our physical and emotional health. Uncovering the cell memories that hold the key to that difference is the quickest, most effective way to change our lives for the better, starting today.

I hope you haven't read the stories in this book feeling excluded, as if traveling back in time to events from this life or past lives takes some special skill on the clients' part, or that these clients are unique in having had past lives to regress to. Every person in this book is as "ordinary" and as "*extra*ordinary" as you are, and I promise you that your rich, eternal history is waiting inside your spirit mind right this minute, waiting to be acknowledged, share its wisdom, and release its pain.

I have never met a person who wouldn't or couldn't return to at least one past life. Not one, in thousands upon thousands of regressions in the last quarter century. So please, I can't stress this enough, know that if you're even slightly curious about experiencing your past, *you can*. It's that simple, and that amazing.

There are three common fears my clients express before a regression, and in case you share these fears, let me ease your mind so that you can read and use this chapter with no reluctance.

- *I don't think I can be hypnotized.* Every client of all the thousands I've worked with has been able to achieve some degree of being "under," whether it's ten percent or ninety percent, and the success of a regression isn't dependent on what that degree is. In fact, as you'll see later in the chapter, while hypnosis is a great pathway to the memories held in our spirit minds and our cells, there are other pathways

to those memories as well, through simple
meditation or your natural ability to visualize.

- *I don't know how to visualize.* It's really a shame
  that visualization has been made by some to
  sound like some complex, esoteric skill that
  can only be accomplished if you're sitting in
  the lotus position wearing crystals and a tur-
  ban. The truth is, every single one of us visual-
  izes dozens of times every day. If you couldn't
  visualize, you'd never be able to picture what
  your loved ones, your home, your pets, a tree,
  the sky, or your workplace look like unless you
  were looking right at them at the time. You'd
  never be able to describe anyone or anything,
  and the only way you'd ever find your car in a
  crowded parking lot is if you waited until every
  other car was gone and then hope your key fits
  in whatever car still happens to be sitting
  there. Visualizing is nothing more than picturing something, and when you're headed back
  to your past, the more detail the better.

- *What if I find out that I was a terrible person in a
  past life?* First of all, if you were a *really* terrible person, you'd be a dark entity, and as I ex-

plained in Part One, dark entities are unable to revisit their past lives, nor do they care to. So the very fact of uncovering a past life in which you were terrible eliminates the possibility of your being beyond hope and estranged from God's unconditional love. Second of all, because we're on earth to learn and to grow, it's guaranteed that we're going to make mistakes, and some of those mistakes are bound to be big ones. I'm on my fifty-fourth lifetime here. Needless to say, not all of those lifetimes have been worthy of medals and testimonial dinners. Like you, I'm sure, I've done some things right, but I've made my share of major mistakes too, in past lives and in this one. Mistakes in any of our lives are only worth hanging our heads about if we refuse to own up to them, do our best to rectify them, pay attention to the lessons woven through them, and demand of ourselves that we not repeat them. And if, in some other lifetime, we committed acts we still haven't forgiven ourselves for and still carry guilt about it in our cell memories, what a waste to live this lifetime in ancient shadows when the sun is within such easy reach.

To show you how accessible past lives and the release of negative cell memory can be, I have to share a letter that arrived in my office on the day I started writing this book. It was from a man named Harry, who, in his words, was "dragged to" one of my Cleveland lectures by his wife. He was tired after a ten-hour work shift, his neck was tight and sore as it always got when he was stressed-out. All he'd had for dinner was a cold drive-through burger and fries on the way to the auditorium, and the last thing on this earth he felt like doing that evening was "sitting and listening to some psychic read tea leaves for a couple of hours." (For the record, I've tried reading tea leaves before. You know what I see when I look at tea leaves? I see the same old meaningless wet tea leaves you do.)

If you've been to my lectures, you know that after the intermission, I lead a group meditation, which is an especially powerful exercise when there are three or four thousand people participating. It starts with relaxation and proceeds from there into the meditation itself, the direction of which depends on the subject of the lecture, or on the general feeling in the room. Sometimes the audience members visit loved ones on The Other Side, sometimes they meet their Spirit Guides, sometimes they simply drop in on a past life, and sometimes I take them to a point of entry for some chronic physical or emotional cell-memory pain and help them release it.

Harry happened to be there one night when I was leading a cell-memory regression. When I directed the audience to sit comfortably with their legs uncrossed, feet flat on the floor and their hands in their laps, palms upward, he said in his letter that "my first thought was, 'good, I could use a quick nap.' But I certainly wasn't about to go along with some silly meditation nonsense I knew nothing about and cared even less." He found himself enjoying the relaxation part because he definitely needed it, which encouraged him to keep listening and doing what he was told as long as it felt good. This encouraged him to listen as I quietly took everyone back through their lives and into the deeper past their spirit minds and cells were still holding.

"Next thing I knew," his letter read, "I was sitting on the back of a horse with my hands tied behind my back and a noose dangling in front of me. There were a lot of men around me, also on horseback, and there was no way to escape. I don't know how I knew this, because no one was saying anything to me, but I was aware that I was about to be hanged for killing a man and that I didn't do it. Then a black hood was put over my head; I felt the noose being slipped around my neck; I heard a slap on my horse's rear end to make it bolt out from under me, and then I was hanging there with just enough breath left in me to realize that my neck was broken."

As I always do during these regression meditations, I ended with the prayer that all the negative cell memories anyone in the room had encountered be released and resolved in the white light of the Holy Spirit, and then I brought everyone back to that time in the auditorium, fully awake and refreshed, and proceeded with questions from the audience.

"When I first came out of the meditation," Harry wrote, "I noticed that my neck had stopped hurting, but I figured it was because of the relaxation exercise you had us do. It's now been four months since that night, though, and after years of suffering on and off with this neck pain I'd given up on curing, it's completely gone. I'm still not convinced that my neck was in pain from my being hanged in a past life, but I am convinced that I'm healed and I have you to thank for it. Now if you can just get my wife to stop saying 'I told you so,' I'll tell everyone I know that you're a miracle worker."

I've received dozens of letters from people who've had some phobia, emotional problem, or physical discomfort disappear after a group meditation at one of my lectures, and I'm pleased to add that not all of those people had to be dragged there.

This is not to say, "Aren't I amazing?" It's just to make the point that you don't have to be hypnotized, you don't have to be skilled at meditation techniques or even know the first thing about them, nor do you have to believe in or have an opinion about the idea of past lives to experience a successful cell-memory healing. I have to admit, there are some amazing aspects to it, too. Cell memory is amazing. The healings are amazing. And most amazing of all is the miraculous combination of God and our open-minded willingness to receive Him that allows those healings to happen.

If, on the other hand, you really feel you'd benefit most from a private hypnosis regression, I'm happy to say that that opportunity is a little more readily available than it was a year or two ago. As I mentioned earlier, the length of my client waiting list for readings horrifies me, and I'll keep trying to find ways to remedy that until I accomplish it, believe me. But while I can't train my staff and my ministers to be psychic, I've trained several of my ministers to become very skilled and gifted certified hypnotists who are doing beautiful regression work. Two of them, Tina Coleman and Linda Potter, have begun traveling throughout the country doing regressions by appointment, and I can't encourage you enough to call my office or visit my Web site, details of which are available at the end of this book, for more information about Tina's and Linda's schedules. I would never endorse them if I hadn't personally taught them and seen them in action, and if I didn't love and trust them with all my heart.

FINDING YOUR OWN WAY BACK

ALL OF THE ABOVE having been said, I want to assure you again that you really can accomplish your own effective, healing regression at your own quiet convenience. You can confine your travel back in time to this lifetime or to any other lifetime you want. You can proceed as quickly or as slowly as your comfort level allows, and you can do your regression in private or with a small group of cooperative loved ones. In the next several pages, I'll be taking you through the journey, with only a few points of clarification before we begin.

The Importance of Lights and Colors

As your healing trip back in time progresses, you'll be asked to visualize different colors of light. The colors aren't randomly chosen. Each of them has its own significance, and the more clearly and vividly you picture the colors as they come up in the meditation, the more effective the experience will be. Make every color glowing, vibrant, alive, as if it has a breath and pulse of its own, so that you can feel a rejuvenating, comforting, calming warmth from its presence.

White is cleansing and purity, the brilliantly sacred light of the Holy Spirit. White light protects us, enveloping us in the grace of God's unconditional love and repelling any darkness that dares to approach it.

Blue is the color of tranquillity and heightened awareness. It opens the mind, the body, the spirit, and the heart to all the positive wisdom we bring with us from our infinite past into this lifetime and drowns out the harsh earthly noise that separates us from the blessed truth of our own immortality.

Green is healing. It invigorates, empowers, and excites. It sends rich blood coursing to every organ, every cell, every living molecule of the body, curing and renewing all it touches on its endless life-giving path.

Gold is the glittering, gorgeous gift of divine dignity, a gift we can carelessly give away but that can never be taken from us against our will. Gold is a head held high, a hand universally extended to offer the same respect it demands, a generous heart so secure in its love for and from its Creator that it can't conceive of being petty or unkind to anyone with whom it shares the courage to spend time on this brief, rough trip away from Home.

Purple holds the key to the past and the future, lifting the fine veil that clouds our view of immortality. The royal purple light links us to our sacred birthright as children of God and, with more resonant clarity than any other color in the spectrum, gives us the swift courage to step into that timeless dimension where our history lies and bravely face all we've been, all we know, and all we have yet to learn as our spirits stretch, reach, and insist on nothing less than the greatest potential God intended. In the glow of purple light, we reverently celebrate the miracle of our sovereign lineage and know to the core of our being that our Mother and Father can hear our thanks for the breath, truth, honor, and meaning to the eternal lives They've given us that we're about to explore.

The Use of Candles

Candles aren't a necessity for a regression, of course, and there isn't a candle in the world that has any power of its own. But in addition to encouraging peace and calm and focus, they make two significant offerings to the atmosphere of sanctity every acknowledgment of the spirit mind and cell memories deserves.

One is the sheer force of the rituals that have preceded us for thousands upon thousands of years, rituals in which candles were treasured elements, cherished reminders of the light of God inside each of us, flames as white and pure as the Holy Spirit they signify. To light a simple candle in God's honor is to re-create a gesture first embraced by our ancestors from more generations ago than we can count and, with that one small act, take our proud place among them.

The other is the lesser known but equally valuable fact that while the spirit world can't see electric lights, they can see and are drawn to candlelight. As we travel back into the history that is ours and ours alone, attracting loved ones, enemies, and other significant beings from other times and places lends a valuable richness to the journey, with the added grace of perspective that transforms knowledge into heartfelt understanding.

Client after client has found candles enormously helpful during regressions, just as I love to include them in my own private meditations. And the meanings of the colors used in the regression can be a guide to the colors of the candles you might want around you for this experience—a white candle for the protective purity of the Holy Spirit, a blue candle to calm you and sensitize your mind to even the smallest details of the journey, a green candle for the healing that will come from releasing the negative cell memories you may encounter, a gold candle to remind you to view every step you've taken and life you've lived with the compassionate dignity of an adult watching a child awkwardly but resolutely learning to walk, and certainly a royal purple candle to represent the Creator, whose unconditional love will keep you safe and always, always sacred, not in spite of your imperfection but because of your courage in confronting it and refusing to settle for anything less than your finest, greatest potential.

Taping and Note-Taking

Rather than straining to remember each step of the meditation and regression, you'll undoubtedly get more value from the experience if you prerecord the italicized sections that follow or have a friend

whose voice is pleasant and calming to you prerecord it for you. I want this whole process to be
about *you*, and the uninterrupted luxury of intensity
that will build and deepen as you proceed. What I
don't want is for you to be just getting some relaxed
momentum going and suddenly have to stop and
say, "Wait, what's next?"

You'll also thank yourself both during and after if
you record your regression as it happens or have a
trusted loved one take notes. It's impossible to set
your spirit mind free and fully indulge in its memories if your conscious mind is poised too close by trying to memorize everything you say. In fact, the more
you can excuse your conscious mind for the duration,
the more complete this experience will be for you.
Just as no client ever leaves my office or hangs up
from a phone reading without a tape of everything
that was said by both of us, I'd hate for you to think
back days or weeks later on your regression and find
that your cluttered, busy, fallible conscious mind has
lost details of it under piles of trivia.

The Observant Position

I'll remind you of this again throughout the regression, because it's very important: while I want you
to feel the full force of every pleasant, happy, loving

moment you encounter along the path through your history, I also want a safe distance between you and anything scary or painful you confront. There's nothing cowardly about refusing to relive it. Assume a "been there, done that" stance, assure yourself that living through it once was quite enough, thank you, and order yourself to "go to the observant position," which simply means standing back and watching the event rather than reexperiencing it. Some regressive hypnotists seem to get an odd satisfaction from watching their subjects writhe around in the agony of a harsh memory. I've never known that kind of intense relived pain to have any worthwhile effect on my clients at all, and if it's not going to help you, why on earth put yourself through it?

So as you proceed with your regression, in addition to the reminders I'll frequently give you, please be confident that you'll immediately know to say and respond to the words, "Go to the observant position," and it will cue you to step away from a hurtful experience from your past and view it with no more involvement than if you were reviewing home movies. If someone is with you when you do your regression, give them that same command to use as well if they see you getting too frightened or upset.

Patience

I can't urge you enough to eliminate any kind of judgment and expectation from your regression exercises. There's no such thing as "good at it" or "bad at it," no such thing as "too fast" or "too slow," no minimum or maximum number of times it "should" take you to "succeed" at this. The simple act of trying *is* succeeding. You'll get some benefit out of every effort, whether you expose and release some long-buried cell memories or just give yourself a few moments of focus and relaxation.

No pressure. No self-consciousness. No nonsense about there being "right" or "wrong" answers. However much or little time you're able to set aside for this, it's all yours. Demand it, claim it, embrace it, and don't you dare spend a single second of it worried that you might "fail." In this glorious process, worrying about failing means worrying about something that happens to be impossible.

The meditation and regression that follow are divided into three separate parts, depending on your own personal goals for the experience. It's important that you do them in the order they're written, but again, take them at your own pace until you're comfortable with each of them. If at any time you get in-

terrupted or your mind wanders to the point where
you can't get it back on track, that's fine. Stop. No
one's grading you on this. My only reminder for
when you try again is not to pick up where you left
off. Start over, remembering that this is a process that
builds gradually. Just like any good workout—and
this is absolutely a workout for your mind and
spirit—it's important to warm up before you even
think about hitting your stride.

The first part is a relaxation exercise. It's wonderful groundwork for the regressions to come, but it
can also stand alone as a lovely, peaceful way to calm
yourself, relieve stress, collect yourself after a hard
day, or prepare yourself for one ahead of time. It can
take as long as you like, or, with practice, just a few
moments. In my dreams, I have an hour or two every
day to devote to relaxing and meditating. In reality,
I'm lucky if I can find a spare five minutes. I know the
same goes for many of you. So take it from me, this
exercise works even if you save it for your morning
shower, walking from your car to your office, or that
space between your head hitting the pillow and actually falling asleep.

Part Two is a journey back into this and only this
lifetime. Some of you have pressing and legitimate
questions about events from this life, and as we've
seen, many of our cell memories, good and bad, are

rooted in the lives we're living now. Others of you aren't necessarily convinced that past lives even exist, and I'm not in the business of trying to drum up converts, no matter how passionately convinced I am in what I believe. In either or both of those cases, you can get enormous value from simply completing Part One and Part Two and leaving it at that.

Part Three is the bridge to your lives before this one, and the secrets of the cell memories those lives are holding. It's a brilliant, fascinating, colorful, and informative journey, whether you take it as fact or purely out of open-mindedly skeptical curiosity. You'll get glimpses of your past that you never dreamed existed, you'll solve some mysteries about yourself and discover others, and you'll see for yourself that while any past lives you uncover did end, not once did you experience a finality we mistakenly call "death."

Whether you explore only Part One, only Parts One and Two or all three, I wish you healing, I wish you a lasting reunion with all the happiness and love you've found since God first breathed life into your sacred, eternal spirit. And from the bottom of my heart, I pray for you: *May any pain and negativity you're holding from the past in your spirit mind and cell memory be released and resolved forever in the white light of the*

Holy Spirit, and may they be replaced with health, joy, and the constant awareness of God's arms around you for the rest of your productive, compassionate, never-ending life.

Relaxation

Lie in a prone position or sit comfortably in a chair, whichever makes you feel more at ease. Loosen or remove anything you're wearing that restricts your breathing and movement in the slightest, or that will distract you in any way. If you choose to lie down, keep your legs uncrossed. If you sit, make sure the soles of your feet are flat on the floor. In either case, let your hands rest lightly on your legs with the palms facing upward, in a position of unclenched openness and your willingness to receive God's grace, energy, and healing.

Let your eyes gently close, excusing yourself from everything around you except the peaceful assurance of these words and the trusted voice that carries them through your hungry conscious mind and into your wise, loved, and loving spirit. Picture the pure white light of the Holy Spirit appearing like a divine veil directly above you, and as you do, take three long, deep breaths: in, then out again, in, then out again, in, then out again. With each inhale the veil of white light draws closer to you until, on the third breath, you feel it settle over you like a warm, smooth blanket of spun silk, covering you with the quiet elation only faith can offer.

Your breathing stays deep and rhythmic as, taking your time, your entire focus moves to your feet. You feel the sole, the arch, each toe, each bone and muscle, and soon you become aware of the life-giving, tension-relieving flow of blood to every cell and pore until with each new breath you take, the soles ease their tightness, the taut muscles in the arches uncoil, every tiny bone in each toe is soothed by the warmth of vibrant circulation until you can almost sense your veins opening wider to gratefully receive the life coursing through them. Pain dissolves. Stress ebbs away. The blessing of health penetrates you like cool rain nourishing parched earth.

Slowly the relief, the release, the warm, calming surge of vitality begins to spread up through your ankles, your calves, the bones of your knees, the long-overlooked muscles of your thighs.

You feel renewal pulsing through every organ, every tendon and muscle, every living cell of the pelvis and stomach. Your spine straightens, tingling with life. Your lungs are cleansed with fresh, clear, sweet-smelling air. Your heart pounds with the strength of a joyful child, and you feel that same strength pumping its heat into your shoulders, down *your arms, into every finger of your hands until they're limp with the relief of this quiet, tender attention.*

The cleansing, surging heat makes its way to your neck and your jaw, where so much of your tension has gathered. One by one, every muscle unwinds and lets go, exhaling, releasing, relaxing, unburdened and at peace. Your mouth feels it too, and goes slack, the tightness gathered there vanishing like a passing shadow, leaving no trace of itself. Your brow eases as if a cool, soft, loving hand is stroking it, and that same hand moves to cover your eyes with God's healing tenderness.

As His hand lingers on your eyes, you use the deepened darkness to envision a starless sky of midnight-blue velvet for as far as you can see. Slowly, in the center of this rich midnight blue, a tiny pinhole of gold light appears. Your focus moves from your tranquil body to this tiny light. You stare at it, mesmerized, knowing it hints of sacred wisdom, the holy dignity of your divine lineage, and absolute proof of the eternity God bestowed at the moment of your creation.

The tiny gold dot of light begins to pulsate, alive, directing the still stronger beat of your heart. Your breath ebbs and flows in time with the light, and with it you begin to detach from every pain you've ever felt, every hurt, every anger, every slight, every injury, physical and emotional, and you know with certainty that you have embraced all the lessons you've learned from that pain, and the rest can leave you now. It's not a part of you, it's of no use or value to you, and you give yourself permission to let it go. The more you feel that pain lift like a harmless vapor from your cells, your body, your mind, and your wise, infinite spirit, the more the tiny golden dot begins to grow, overflowing with life, larger and larger, directly above you, its rays dancing in joyful celebration of the Creator you share.

Suddenly, silently, the now huge, glowing, pulsating light explodes against the midnight-blue sky, heavenly fireworks of gold, sending a glittering shower of stars that float like a heated, healing, soothing golden powder onto your face, your hair, your shoulders, your arms, your feet, every pore and cell of your skin, until you glisten with vitality, your body reborn, your spirit cleansed and revived for the challenges that brought it here, strong, brave, and inspired as it continues into the timeless future, into the timeless past, wherever God's sacred hand leads it to find its highest, most loving destiny.

The Journey Back Into This Lifetime

Your skin still glitters from its shower of stars, your body is exhilarated with power and energy, and your mind is as clear and limitless as the cloudless sky that's turning from midnight blue to the quietly thrilling pastels of dawn. You turn from where you stand and find yourself facing a thick forest of rich green trees, as far as you can see.

Your eyes are still closed as you move them upward as if you're focusing on the bridge of your nose, just for a few seconds, a count of five. It sends you deeper into your spirit mind, where a wealth of memories and wisdom lie waiting for you to rediscover them.

You relax your eyes again and find that in those brief moments, the trees have parted, opening up to a beautiful, narrow, endless path at your feet that leads into the forest. You hesitate. But the fragrance of pine, the shafts of golden sunlight glistening through the lush green leaves, and the growing realization that the path doesn't seem completely unfamiliar compel you forward. The white light of the Holy Spirit glows brighter around you as you ask for the courage to walk this path without fear and learn its lessons with all the loving, compassionate patience God has given you.

You step forward, disappearing into glorious privacy among the thick green trees, and within moments you find yourself in a quiet clearing where a scene from your twentieth year in this lifetime is in progress in perfect, intricate detail. And you, suddenly twenty years old, step into it. If no scene or moment appears immediately, be patient. Wait, reassure yourself that once upon a time, you were, in fact, twenty, and ask yourself what was going on in your life at that age. Was there a first day at a new job, a birthday, a Christmas, a college party, an apartment you lived in, that stands out in your mind? If nothing still appears, relax. It will come at its own pace, maybe triggered by a detail as small as a car you owned then, or a favorite movie or song or sport or television show, that will allow the rest of the scene to unfold. You look around, noticing every color, every smell, every face, what you're wearing, the style of your hair, and most of all, how you feel. If the memory is happy, or if you simply notice that you feel healthy and young, relive it, embrace it, be infused with it. If the memory upsets you in any way, or if at twenty you were having physical or mental health problems that are playing out in front of you, just *observe without letting the scene penetrate your psyche. As you stand there, aware of your powerful ability to access your past, offer a prayer: "All the vitality, peace, and security my cells remember from my twentieth year, let them stay with me and renew my body and spirit today and always. But any negativity, conscious or unconscious, that has burdened me from the age of twenty, let it be resolved into the white light of the Holy Spirit that surrounds me, today, tomorrow, and throughout my happy, healthy, productive, innovative, spiritual life."*

You step away from that scene and back onto the forest path, walking on with increasing strength and courage, rejuvenated by your visit to your twentieth year. The sun's golden rays dance through the healing green that brushes gently against your warm, bare arms, urging you along. You bask in the beauty around you, in no hurry. Birds sing nearby, you're safe and protected and peaceful, and there is nowhere else you would rather be at this quiet, graceful moment. Another clearing appears, and you move confidently toward it.

A scene from your tenth year has been perfectly preserved, waiting for you to arrive, and in a heartbeat or two, you're ten years old again. A different birthday, a different Christmas, a best friend, a first day of school, your bedroom, your favorite pet, a music lesson, some event, no matter how trivial, is there for you, as real as the day it happened. Again, if nothing comes, be patient and let your conscious mind help you. What did your school look like? Where did you live? What grade were you in? Who was your teacher? What was your favorite subject, or your favorite game at re- cess? What was your favorite food, or your favorite toy? Any detail, even the tiniest one, is all you need to make the scene spring to life and to become as much or as little a part of it as your peace of mind dictates. Explore. Notice everything. Any happiness is yours to keep with you, and any pain or sadness is yours only for the value of reminding you that you were strong and resilient enough to survive it. You thank God for all of it, the happiness you celebrated and the pain you learned from and survived, and then, after thanking Him, you continue the prayer: "All the vitality, peace, and security my cells remember from my tenth year, let them stay with me and renew my body and spirit today and always. But any negativity, conscious or unconscious, that has bur- dened me from the age of ten, let it be resolved into the white light of the Holy Spirit that surrounds me, today, to- morrow, and throughout my happy, healthy, productive, in- novative, spiritual life."

After lingering as long as you like, you leave and move on along the path, becoming more energized and excited with every step, these reunions and discoveries fascinating you and any past, needless burdens gone. You know you're safe, you know you'll be protected no matter what, you know God's hand is holding yours and He won't let you fall. You become aware of what lies ahead in the next clearing, and your pace quickens. Your conscious mind would have scoffed at it as impossible, but your spirit mind is completely in charge now: unstoppable, yearning for its history, knowing the conscious mind proclaims all sorts of miracles impossible and then has to stand by in awed, humbled silence when those same miracles become real.

At the next clearing lies the moment of your conception, the moment when your spirit entered the womb from which this life's body will be born. Just as it remembers everything else that's ever happened to it, your spirit can access this memory, too. Don't let yourself think. Simply accept the imagery that comes. And with patience, it will come. You may not be completely confident of that, but you are curious, and you can't resist at least a glance into that clearing that now waits just beyond these last few trees.

You see nothing but darkness at first, so you step farther into the clearing. A gentle wind nudges into each other the branches of the trees behind you, and, without fear, you find you're completely surrounded by that darkness. You're floating, safe, with no sound intruding except the tiny, reassuring beat of your perfect heart. Finally you can make out your impossibly small hands, your impossibly small little limbs and feet moving like shadows in all that darkness. You know where you are. You know you asked to be here. You know you're on just a brief trip away from Home and that soon you'll be thrust into this rough, flawed world called earth again. In your very last moment on The Other Side before you left, you felt the touch of God like a loving kiss on

your forehead, and, Homesick already but braced for
new adventure you chose and charted, you pray: "All the
tality, peace, and security my cells remember from The Other
Side, let them stay with me and renew my body and spirit
today, through my birth and always. But any negativity,
conscious or unconscious, I'm carrying with me, let it be resolved into the white light of the Holy Spirit that is my sacred companion in this close, safe womb, today, tomorrow,
and throughout my happy, healthy productive, innovative,
spiritual life. Amen."

Journey

ast Lives

You linger unafraid in the darkness until you suddenly become aware of the presence of a brilliant purple light behind you. You turn to face it and find it to be so bright, so powerful, and so all-encompassing that it blinds you to everything else around you. But it is also compelling, full of love and wisdom and ultimate compassion. In awe, knowing you're safe, you step toward it and through it, joyful at the sense of God's tangible presence in that rich, sacred, impossibly loving purple glow.

A tunnel opens in the heart of the purple light. In the glow you can see inside its gleaming etched golden walls, intricate and beautiful, calming and still. Your feet eagerly cross the threshold, and instantly you're moving, gliding through this gorgeous tunnel, and you realize you're traveling back in time, past that moment of conception you experienced earlier, farther and farther back, beyond other lives *and events your spirit has already resolved, as a voice inside you says, "Go to the point of entry of your most pressing cell-memory pain." You understand perfectly.*

The same magnificent purple light that sent you on your way at the beginning of the tunnel greets you at its end, illuminating a vast, brightly colored map of the world. That same voice inside you says, "Wherever my first point of entry occurred, through the grace of my cell memory and my spirit mind toward their desire to be healed, may my hand find that place on this map." Without thinking about it or even looking at the map, let your hand be guided by your spirit to touch the map. Then look to see that specific point where your finger has landed and, with faith and acceptance, say, "I willingly ask my spirit to take me to this significant place it remembers and see the life and time I spent there."

Your spirit mind, free and powerful, obliges, and in an instant, you're there, back in time to a whole other life that was once yours, as real as the life from which you're taking this brief break. You look around to get your bearings, too fascinated to be cautious or afraid.

As you familiarize yourself with this reality you're remembering, your conscious mind will pay attention without intruding, and the answers to all the questions you ask are immediate, without judgment, without editing. There is no wrong answer. The first words out of your mouth are all that count.

Where are you?

Do you know your first or last name? If not, it doesn't matter.

How old are you?

Are you male or female?

What do you look like? Are you tall? Short? Slender? Stocky? What color is your skin, your hair, your eyes? What clothing are you wearing, if any? If you have trouble getting a clear image of yourself, find a way to see your reflection, in a mirror, or a glass storefront, or a pond or stream, or a piece of metal, or a window, and simply describe in detail what you see.

What year is this?

Where do you live?

Do you live alone?

If not, who lives with you? Is there anyone around you whom you know in the life from which you're taking this hiatus? Who were those people to you then, and who are they to you now?

Are you healthy, or unhealthy?

If you're unhealthy, what is your illness or injury? When did it begin?

Is this a happy life, or an unhappy one?

If it's happy, what makes it happy? If it's unhappy, what makes it unhappy?

What is your life theme for this lifetime?

What is the best part of this life you're living?

What is the worst?

You chose this moment you're visiting, out of a whole timeless, eternal history, to reveal the point of entry for your most difficult cell memory. What is it about this moment, this circumstance, or this event that had such a profound impact on you? What led to it, and what is essential for you to understand about it?

Again, this is no time for editing or judging. Just talk. Say anything and everything that occurs to you. Your spirit mind has been waiting a very long time for this chance to unburden itself and, as a result, send messages of healing to the cells of your body.

Whenever you're ready, and not until, I want you to be-gin to ease forward in this past life you're reliving. Where were you a year after this point of entry? Five years? Ten years? As long as that particular life continued?

Now I want you to go to those moments before your "death" in that life. First and foremost, notice that all your fears about death meaning annihilation are unfounded, be-cause even though you're watching yourself "die" in a past life, you're still here to see it years, decades, even centuries later, and you're still you.

Once that point has become undeniably clear to you, look at that "death" itself. If it's too frightening or painful, just observe it like a good, objective reporter.

What illness or injury is causing this death?

Where are you?

Who, if anyone, is around you?

Are you reluctant, or glad, to be leaving this lifetime?

In those last moments, are you conscious of the joyful reality that you're about to go Home to The Other Side?

And now, just as the tunnel begins to appear to take you Home, I want you to make everything about that instant stand perfectly still, as if you're executing a "freeze-frame" on a video camera, and offer this prayer:

"Dear God, I thank You for the courage to face that moment in this long-ago life when my spirit mind and the cells of this body took on a burden I've struggled with ever since. At this moment of my death in that same life, please let that burden and all other negativity I'm carrying be resolved in the blessed white light of the Holy Spirit, then, now, and always, so that I can devote my joyful, eternal, unburdened freedom to Thy service for the rest of the happy, healthy, productive, innovative, spiritual life You've given me."

Finally, when you're ready to return, I want you to travel back into this current body and this current life on the slow count of three, relaxed, at your peak of health, faith, and peace of mind, the weight lifted from your spirit mind so that it can cleanse your cells of all remaining darkness and soar with God's love forever.

One. Your eyes slowly open.

Two. Refreshed, and radiant with vitality, you raise your head.

Three. Fully awake and completely renewed, proceed from this moment forward, thanking yourself and God for

the new beginning you've given yourself by opening your
mind and heart to the hidden secrets of cell memory.

The three steps of this meditation can be used for any number of purposes and can be varied to include any imagery that's close to your heart and helps make the trip back in time as real for you as possible. You might want to explore special talents you've had in past lives. You might want to revisit your first day after being born. You might want to go into a past life to see when, where, and how you've known a current loved one, or a current enemy, before.

But I really encourage you to start with this cleansing, renewing exercise, and to repeat some version of it once or twice a month. Cell memory is powerful. It can work for you or against you, and that choice is yours, which makes you more powerful than cell memory can ever be. All you have to do is be aware that it exists, and where it came from, and then, with God's help, cleanse the negative, embrace the positive, and almost immediately, I promise you, notice how much more you're enjoying every day of the adventure of this life you chose.

THE SENTINEL

Once you're free from the physical and emotional burdens your cell memory has been carrying, you'll want to stay free and guard against any new illness and other negativity that might try to interfere with your newfound well-being. One of the easiest, least time-consuming ways to accomplish that is with a visualization my Spirit Guide, Francine, taught me, which she calls the Sentinel.

The Sentinel is simply the image of a person, male or female, whichever you prefer, a foot or so tall, armed for battle, standing watch directly in front of your solar plexus, from your sternum to your abdomen. The image I use is that of a male, dressed as a gladiator, with a shield, helmet, and spear of gold and clothing of purple, standing at attention—a symbolic guardian, glowing in the white light of the Holy Spirit. I take a few moments several times a day to visualize this image.

You can summon the Sentinel whenever you want, just by closing your eyes and picturing him or her in place, sword drawn and ready to defeat any and all negativity around you. But the Sentinel is especially effective after your cell-memory cleansing meditation, when you're at your strongest, purest, healthiest, and most energized. The Sentinel can be your best-kept secret, yours to create as a reminder that God, your Spirit Guide, your Angels, and the spirits of your loved ones from this and every other life you've lived help and protect you each minute of each new day, and all you have to do is notice.

And joining the Sentinel and the rest of that sacred army, please know that with every exquisite, newly liberated step you take through the rest of your happy, healthy, productive, innovative, spiritual life, my most heartfelt prayers are with you.

The Benediction:
A Prayer for Healing

Dear Mother and Father God,

I ask for your blessing to become of sound mind, stalwart of soul, and strong in physical body that I myself am a Trinity that mirrors the Trinity. In doing so I pick up each crucible, each cup, and fill it to the top, that my physical body will be well. The well, the water that springs from the eternal fountain which is Azna, the Mother God. As a mother nurtures her child, so does Mother Azna nurture me.

I will be well; I will be fit; and I will be strong in mind, body, spirit, and higher soul mind.

Nothing will invade. No darkness will invade my mind.

I will have a Sentinel figure that will guard against any illness, germs, fevers, any malignancies.

I will be of sound body, mind, and soul until the very end of my life, and then, with dignity, I will retreat back to my Home.

I ask for protection by the love from Father and Mother God that the Holy Spirit, each day, will descend upon me. And that love which is so strong will protect me from any slings and arrows that may come from any darkness that invades.

If I am already of ill health, I will negate it. I will put myself in the hands of the Blessed Azna to cradle me, to make me well, to make me sound and whole.

If I am carrying any malady from a past life, let it be released now in the white light of the Holy Spirit that surrounds me.

I ask this in the Name of the Father, Mother, Holy Spirit, and Son.

Amen.

About the Author

Sylvia Browne has been working as a psychic for almost half a century. She is the author of *Blessings from The Other Side*, as well as the #1 *New York Times* bestsellers *The Other Side and Back* and *Life on The Other Side*.

You can find out more about Sylvia Browne through her Web site: www.sylvia.org

There is nothing more fascinating, more intensely personal and more uniquely ours than the voyages our minds and spirits take while we sleep. These dreams and other adventures confuse us, alarm us, preoccupy us, relieve us, amuse us, comfort us, inform us, enlighten us and, above all, keep us more sane and whole than we could ever hope to be without them. Our sleep journeys, even the nightmares, are gifts, our allies, to embrace rather than dread, and worth every effort it takes to unravel their mysteries and cherish every valuable lesson they have to offer.

I've been studying the worlds of sleep and dreams for more than thirty years. In the course of those studies I've read a lot of the same dream interpretation material you probably have, and often come away feeling more confused when I finished than I was when I started. Some "experts" swear that there's great cosmic significance in every dream, if we were only bright enough to figure it out. Others are convinced that dreams are nothing but meaningless little vaudeville shows to keep us entertained while we sleep. Still others strain to find sexual symbolism in each tiny detail of our dreams (I'd love to have met Sigmund Freud just once, just long enough to say, "What's *wrong* with you?"), while a few geniuses even insist that the minute we doze off, we disintegrate into any number of vapor blobs and go darting around the universe for reasons I can't figure out for the life of me.

I might have thrown up my hands and dismissed the whole subject of dreams as being too confusing to conquer if it hadn't been for some basic realities I wasn't confused about at all:

First and foremost, I grew up with my Grandmother Ada, a brilliant psychic and teacher who shared her passion for dreams, especially prophetic ones, with her adoring granddaughter and taught me that the subconscious mind understands their meaning whether the conscious mind can make sense of them or not.

Then there was my own passion for world religions, which led me to read and reread every great sacred work and to appreciate how prominently dreams are woven into the exquisite fabric of every one of them. How could I ignore the importance of dreams when there are 121 references to them in the Bible alone?

In addition, maybe because I was born psychic, I devoured the books of all the great psychics, from Edgar Cayce to Arthur Ford to Ruth Montgomery, in the hope of not feeling quite so out of place. At the same time, endlessly curious about exactly how the human mind operates (thinking I could *learn* to be "normal," I guess), I read and studied every book and course I could find on the subjects of psychiatry, psychology and hypnosis, even becoming a master hypnotist in the process and forming lifelong friendships with some of the finest psychiatrists and psychologists in the country. I'm sure there are some members of the psychiatric community who won't appreciate hearing this, but the truth is, the psychic world and the psychiatric world have a lot in common, including a deep interest in uncovering and understanding the secrets hidden in dreams.

Once my career as a psychic was under way, more and more clients were asking for my help with interpreting their dreams. In most situations, I don't mind a bit saying the words, "I don't know." But when clients want and need something from me, I owe them better than a shrug and a simple, "Beats me." So it was for my clients' benefit as well as my own insatiable curiosity that I made it my business to unravel the mysteries of dreams as best I could, to the point where for many years I had the pleasure of teaching very successful dream interpretation classes to the growing number of clients who were as fascinated as I was.

And then one day I found myself so shaken by a dream that I

went to one of my professors for help, and the value of decoding a message received in dreams hit home as it never had before. It was during a period of huge personal upheaval in my life, which, by the way, is when our sleep adventures tend to be more vivid, intense and meaningful than ever. I was juggling my two full-time careers, as both a psychic and a schoolteacher, taking an advanced hypnosis class and, most of all, in the midst of a nasty divorce from my first husband, Gary (technically my second, but that's another story for another book). There was no dispute over money or property, since neither Gary nor I had any money or property to fight over. But there was a huge, ugly dispute over the custody of our two precious little sons, Paul and Chris, and our beautiful foster daughter, Mary, and I wasn't about to let anyone on this earth separate me from my children, *period*. It was a painful, terrifying time that I can still feel in the pit of my stomach as I write about it now, thirty years later.

In my dream, at the height of my fear, I was standing in a classroom, tightly holding my three children—Paul, Chris and Mary—who were huddled beside me, the four of us in the center of a protective circle I'd drawn on the floor. Several androgynous, nonthreatening figures wearing faceless green masks were walking single file around the outside of the circle chanting, "Beware of the three, beware of the three," over and over again. The figures themselves didn't frighten me, but their repeated warning did, and I woke feeling helpless and more afraid than I'd ever felt in my life.

I was awake and almost frantic the rest of that night trying to make sense of what "beware of the three" could possibly mean. What "three" was I supposed to beware of? Surely it wasn't the three innocent children I was trying so fiercely to protect. Was it an upcoming date for a custody hearing that wasn't going to go well for us, maybe the "third" of the month, or "three" months later? Had my estranged husband somehow manufactured "three" charges against me to try to convince the judge that I was an unfit mother? Most unthinkable of all, was I getting a premonition to emotionally brace myself because I was going to lose these "three" children, which I'm not at all sure I could have survived? I must have come up with a thousand possibilities that night while I paced around the house like a lunatic, but none of them felt quite right, let alone offering the kind of help a warning like that should give. I've always said, I'll vigilantly beware of an enemy, I'll bravely square off with an enemy, but I can't do a thing unless I know what or who the enemy is.

Luckily, I was studying advanced hypnosis at the time, and my professor was a genius about the workings of the subconscious mind, including the messages it sends through dreams, and I still count him among my most trusted and insightful colleagues. I was waiting outside his office when he arrived that morning. I was so frantic by then that I hope I didn't grab him by the lapels, but I can't swear I didn't. He patiently led me to the chair beside his desk and simply said, "Tell me what's wrong."

I filled him in on the fierce custody battle that was consuming my life and then described my dream, in all its disturbing detail. I don't cry often, especially in front of other people. I cried that morning.

"You wouldn't think a psychic of all people would feel this helpless," I told him, "but as you know, I'm not one bit psychic about myself. If that dream was trying to tell me something and I blow this custody case because I didn't understand the message, I'll never forgive myself. What am I missing, John? What could 'beware of the three' possibly mean?"

His smile was patient and compassionate. "Tell me," he said, "who's fighting against you for custody? Who's trying to take your children away from you?"

That was easy. "My husband, his mother and, believe it or not, *my* mother."

Instead of pointing out the obvious, he let me catch on all by myself. It took me a few seconds, but finally I added, "In other words, three people. Three people I need to beware of." I was hit with that wave of relief that comes when you know something right and true has just been uncovered. The dream wasn't some dire prediction. It wasn't teasing me with mysterious new information in a kind of infuriating guessing game. It was simply clarifying and reminding me to stay focused on the three people who were conspiring to use my children to hurt me.

I felt as if the weight of the world had been lifted off my shoulders as I left John's office that morning. The fear that had kept me awake and pacing most of the night was replaced by a sense of resolved power, like when you turn on a bright light and discover that the terrifying, shadowy monster in the corner of your bedroom is nothing but a pile of clothes on a chair. My lawyer and I paid even closer attention to "the three" from that day on and, because we did, we won. I was awarded full custody of my children. Thank God.

If any one event sealed my commitment to explore the world of sleep and make its magic more available and understandable to my clients and to myself, it was that dream, its aftermath and everything I learned from the experience.

I learned that there's valuable clarity to be found while we sleep if we can just master the vocabulary to translate it.

I learned firsthand how lost, confused and often frightened my clients felt when they came to me for help with their dreams, and I promised God and myself I would do everything in my power not to let them down.

I learned how important objectivity is when trying to figure out the purpose of a dream, and how easy it is for the conscious mind to overcomplicate a dream's meaning when very often the simplest answer is the right one.

I learned, above all, that the sleep world is richer, more varied and far more vast than I ever imagined and that, as we'll explore in the course of this book, dreams are only the beginning of that world.